Death Now

Death Now

CHRONICLES OF INTELLECTUAL LIFE, 1944

MAURICE BLANCHOT

Translated by Michael Holland

FORDHAM UNIVERSITY PRESS

New York 2019

Cet ouvrage, publié dans le cadre d'un programme d'aide à la publication, bénéficie de la participation de la Mission Culturelle et Universitaire Française aux Etats-Unis, service de l'Ambassade de France aux EU.

This work, published as part of a program of aid for publication, received support from the Mission Culturelle et Universitaire Française aux Etats-Unis, a department of the French Embassy in the United States.

Cet ouvrage a bénéficié du soutien des programmes d'aide à la publication de l'Institut français.

This work, published as part of a program of aid for publication, received support from the Institut Français.

Library of Congress Cataloging-in-Publication Data available online at https://catalog.loc.gov.

Printed in the United States of America

21 20 19 5 4 3 2 1

First edition

Contents

Death Now

Introduction

MICHAEL HOLLAND

With his reputation as a challenging and original novelist already assured, the appearance of *Faux pas* in December 1943 established Blanchot as one of the foremost literary critics of the period.[1] Yet, his first chronicle of 1944, "The Mystery of Criticism," is far from being a celebration of the activity it describes. In fact, the piece is more of a denunciation: Criticism, he argues, is ignorant of what it is, what it wants, and what it achieves. Its very existence is therefore open to doubt. In terms that indicate his closeness to Georges Bataille, Blanchot goes on to argue that poets and novelists have the task of preserving language by sacrificing it. They endow language with supreme value in the very process of destroying it. This is a theme that has been gradually developed in the years during which he has been writing these chronicles.[2] But the critic is not simply the chronicler of this process of destruction. He also provides it with its purest expression; he is a poet who refuses to write poetry, a novelist who refuses the novel, and he thus takes destruction beyond the generic bounds that literature imposes on it. If his is therefore the supreme mode in which literature performs its purifying task, it is because he ultimately refuses in turn even to be a critic: Silence is the only mode in which he can write. This may be a desperate ambition, Blanchot concludes, it is nonetheless rich in significance.

Success left Blanchot in a sort of limbo at the beginning of 1944. Far from confirming him in his position as a novelist and a critic, recognition appears to have convinced him of the futility of both the disciplines in which he had made his name. He has described how reluctant he was to turn his literary chronicles into a book, and, following the appearance of *Aminadab* in 1942, he published no further volume of fiction until 1948.[3] Between January and August 1944, he confined himself to sending his weekly chronicle down to the *Journal des Débats* in Clermont-Ferrand. But as the inaugural article makes clear, everything he wrote was merely a substitute for the silence that henceforth lay at the heart of his writerly activity. That activity itself was now curtailed. In 1944 his chronicles became significantly shorter than hitherto, and the proportion made up of direct quotation displayed a marked increase.[4] What is more, the *Journal des Débats* was now a ghost of its former self, staffed by a few die-hard *Pétainistes* and read by almost no one.[5] To publish there was to go practically unnoticed.[6] Following his final chronicle on August 17, the writer's silence that Blanchot evoked in his very first chronicle in 1941 became a reality for him.[7] He would not publish anything more until July 1945.[8]

Other than these chronicles, there are few other traces of Blanchot's literary life in 1944. He was a member of the jury of the Prix de la Pléiade, which was founded in July 1943 and awarded its first prize to Mouloudji's novel *Enrico* in February 1944. There is no available account of how the vote took place that year. Significantly, at the one literary event where Blanchot's presence is recorded, it is his *silence* that has left a trace; during a "Discussion on Sin" that took place in March 1944, Georges Bataille presented a paper entitled "Summit and Decline" that met with considerable hostility. As Michel Surya observes, rather than intervene to defend Bataille, who was caught in the crossfire from both the Catholics and the Sartreans present, Blanchot said nothing. Surya appears surprised, not to say offended, by this; he finds it inexcusable that someone whose responses to the public readings of what will become *Inner Experience* shaped Bataille's thinking should have in effect abandoned his friend, leaving him alone, with no one to rely on.[9] Yet, as Jean Lescure recounts in his history of the journal *Messages*, at a meeting of Bataille's "Collège socratique" in 1943, Blanchot sat silently apart from everyone else, his intervention reduced to a single gnomic utterance that prompted the assembled company to disperse.[10] Unlike Chateaubriand, unable to face the silence that arose from the "pure vacancy, the desperate nudity" to which his self-imposed exile in Geneva exposed him,[11] it is clear that Blanchot espoused that silence in every aspect of his life as a writer during the occupation years.

Almost nothing is known either about what Blanchot's life had become more generally by 1944. As a former journalist, he doubtless continued to pay close attention to daily events. But the state of voluntary absence from all external activity that he described in a letter to Francis Ambrière in 1943 would seem to endure.[12] In another letter to Ambrière, dated March 1944, he observed, "now that the outcome cannot be changed, there is a fear of what the ultimate upheaval will bring: people want it to happen as easily as if it were by miracle. Fortunately, such faintheartedness is not found in everyone."[13] If these words appear to suggest an informed sympathy for active resistance, no hard evidence yet exists that Blanchot was involved with any of the established Resistance movements. In his biography, Christophe Bident states that he drove members of the secret army across the Swiss border and points to references in work by Claude Roy and Roger Laporte and (presumably) to Denise Rollin's correspondence, all to the effect that Blanchot did engage in resistance activity.[14] Blanchot himself refers to "comrades from the maquis" in *The Instant of My Death*,[15] and it is easy to imagine that his closeness to Jean Paulhan during the

Occupation years must have made him privy to some of Paulhan's sympathies and involvements, even though it was not on the *Lettres Françaises* side that Blanchot had to do with him, but on the *NRF* side (where what mattered was not taking sides).

Like many writers, Blanchot withdrew from Paris as the war entered its last phase to spend more and more time in his family homes in Chalons and Quain. Increasingly, writers were becoming the targets of repression, particularly if they were Jews. The poet Max Jacob was sent to Drancy in February and died there the following month; Robert Desnos was arrested in February and sent to Buchenwald and then Theresienstadt, where he died in June 1945; Benjamin Fondane was arrested in March and sent from Drancy to Auschwitz in May, dying there in October; Marc Bloch, also arrested in March, was shot in June. In May, the wife of Marcel Jouhandeau denounced Jean Paulhan to the Gestapo, obliging him to go into hiding. Blanchot claimed that he himself was denounced to the Gestapo during the Occupation by the editors of *Je suis partout*, and that this almost cost him his life.[16] Even the provinces offered no guarantee of safety. On June 29, he narrowly escaped execution in reprisal for resistance activity near Quain.[17]

If Blanchot remained aloof from what was happening all around him in 1944, his weekly chronicles appear to give a mixed picture of where his sympathies lay. Sometimes his choice of author appears to express solidarity with victims of violent oppression. In January, he reviews a novel by Louis Parrot, a resistance writer, and on April 27, the subject of his chronicle is a book by Louis-Martin Chauffier, the director of the clandestine newspaper *Libération*, who was arrested by the Gestapo the following month and sent to Belsen. And on July 27 he quotes from a poem by Robert Desnos, who had died in Theresienstadt in June. In other chronicles, however, he appears indifferent to the political leanings of the authors he discusses and to those of their publishers. While he regularly selects books from his own publisher, Gallimard, he also reviews new works published by Stock, Grasset, and Denoël, notwithstanding the fact that all three were placed on an "Index" of undesirable publishers in April and again in July 1944.[18] This would not necessarily be significant: Stock and Denoël also published authors with no political leanings, such as Marcel Arland and Dominique Rolin, and Blanchot reviewed books by each of them. Meanwhile, the book by Ramon Fernandez, a known collaborator, that Blanchot reviews in "The Mystery of Criticism" was published by the Éditions du Pavois, which would become one of the foremost publishing houses in the postwar years. If Blanchot's attitude toward the literature of the time does not reflect the polarization present in France, this is less a sign of his aloofness than a reflection of the attitude of publishers themselves. And this had its counterpart in general cultural attitudes during the Occupation. While resistance and collaboration both had their unconditional adherents in the literary world, many writers kept up relations across the hostile divide.[19] More or less explicitly at the heart of this attitude lay a version of the absolute priority given to cultural relations that informed Blanchot's outlook from the outset. However, Blanchot's position displays none of the complacencies or occasional dangers of such a stance. If literature had once allowed a sense of shared cultural values to blur political boundaries, by offering writers a sense of community that the occupation had destroyed, it had now become the consummation of that destruction in Blanchot's eyes. If it permitted a detachment from events in the world, this was not a retreat into a domain that not even disaster could destroy; its detachment was the mode in which disaster occurred.

One chronicle in particular from 1944 illustrates this clearly. "Fantastic Novels" begins by examining *Prelude to Apocalypse* by Robert Poulet, which was published by Denoël. For once, author and publisher fell under the same suspicion: Robert Poulet, whose brother Georges became one of the foremost postwar literary critics, was the political director of the collaborationist Belgian newspaper *Le Nouveau Journal*, for which activity he was condemned to death in 1945. His political position was no secret to anyone, and it is precisely for publishing books such as his that Denoël was judged undesirable. For Blanchot to review a book by such a compromised figure would at first sight appear to compromise him. In fact, however, Blanchot was drawn to the book on account of neither its author nor its publisher, but because of its subject. The Apocalypse was a major source of inspiration for his first novel, *Thomas the Obscure*, especially its earlier versions. But "compared to the war," Blanchot argues, "apocalypse has something faintly banal about it" in Poulet's hands. He finds much that is interesting in the book, but there is something missing, namely what Blanchot calls "the human condition," which, at the present time, takes the form of "circumstances that literature can still neither express directly nor even distort." What exactly were these circumstances?

As the end of the war approached, the situation in France became increasingly violent. Allied bombing raids increased in intensity.[20] At the beginning of 1944, Joseph Darnand's Milice was transformed into an increasingly powerful and active force, with a mission to eliminate Jews and repress resistance activity.[21] It set up its own courts-martial, where summary justice was meted out to members of the Resistance, whose violent activity intensified in retaliation. As the months went by and German defeat appeared more and more inevitable, a cycle of terror and counterterror took hold of France, leading commentators then and since to argue that the country was descending into a state of civil war.[22] The days of Germany's domination of Europe might well appear numbered, for most people the outcome of the war remained hidden from view behind seemingly never-ending chaos.

The political situation in France was now extraordinary, not to say unique. The Vichy regime remained the nominal government, but after the German occupation of the whole of the country in November 1942, its authority was increasingly weakened. In parallel, a provisional government was gradually emerging from the Free French movement in London and the

Commandement Civil et Militaire in Algiers. On June 3, 1943, these two movements fused to form the Comité Français de Libération Nationale, and exactly one year later, on June 3, 1944, it declared itself to be the provisional government of the French Republic, with authority over the whole of France. It was immediately recognized by most European states. Two forms of sovereignty were now vying for control of France, the one with a brave optimism to which postwar France owes its existence, the other with a deluded commitment to a doomed ideal. Yet, despite the ideological and historical differences between them, these two regimes had one thing in common: For both, real power lay elsewhere. If that is self-evident in the case of the provisional government based in London, it was equally the case for the Vichy government, whose official title was L'État Français, the French State. A state, in Max Weber's definition, "claims the monopoly of the legitimate use of physical force within a given territory."[23] That is the condition of its existence and the basis of its power. By invading France in 1940 and installing a puppet regime, the Germans suspended political power and replaced it with force. The French State created by Vichy was therefore founded on an illusion. Far from being "the sole source of the 'right' to use violence,"[24] as Weber's definition continues, the power it exercised derived entirely from the violent invasion of its territory by Germany. For as long as the French—and the world—gave credence to the Vichy regime, the illusion was maintained. By 1944, it had begun to crumble on every side. In circumstances that prevail only during revolutions, the French thus found themselves in the extraordinary situation of being the subjects of two opposed yet equally unreal regimes, each deploying the full apparatus of state power, yet neither able to exercise it for as long as Germany occupied France by force. Now, in the unstable vacuum created by this political interregnum, force itself began to falter, the order it imposed became unstable: Violence and counter-violence on the part of the partisans of each regime (the Milice, the Resistance) increasingly invaded everyday life, while the occupant resorted to violent acts that were increasingly excessive and uncontrolled.[25]

From a historical perspective, it would be little more than an abstraction to bestow meaning on this moment of total conflict. In retrospect, it fits neatly into the story of France's liberation and Germany's defeat. Yet it and it alone gives coherence to Maurice Blanchot's intellectual position in 1944. It is henceforth "the human condition" that he referred to, and as a writer, he will never move beyond it. In the early years of occupation, Blanchot believed it was possible to preserve the reality of France by defending its culture during what Jean Guéhenno called "the sort of swoon [*syncope*]" into which the nation had fallen.[26] Formally speaking, he paid allegiance as many writers did to a third "France," as unreal as those of Vichy and the Resistance but, unlike them, knowingly grounded in the unreality of a timeless ideal.[27] After the failure of "Jeune France" and the demise of the *Nouvelle Revue Française*, he could no longer ignore what his prewar journalism had gradually revealed to him: The "swoon" was not a temporary state. France and with it the entire national structure it epitomized was riven by contradiction; concealed beneath the illusion represented by Vichy lay not *la France éternelle*,[28] but turmoil and chaos.[29] If literature alone survived this total disaster, it was not because it was the last bastion of French sovereignty, but because in "a world in ruins" it was now the only sovereignty that remained. As he wrote in "The Mystery of Criticism," when literature destroys language, "what disappears acquires extreme value, shatters the specific realities that define it and gives form to absolute sovereignty." In the violent hiatus that holds political sovereignty in suspense, all that endures is the self-sacrificing sovereignty of language as literature. Now therefore, literature cannot simply provide an apocalyptic afterimage of ruin. If language in a state of absolute division against itself appears to reflect the violence and counterviolence into which political sovereignty has collapsed, it is unable to provide a signifier for that collapse because it is contemporaneous with it: Politics and literature share a moment that has fallen outside of time, and they coexist in what Blanchot will later term "the abyss of the present."[30] The "absolute sovereignty" of ruin to which literature gives form subsumes and perpetuates the violence into which the world has sunk. Literature is consciousness *as* disaster, not consciousness *of* it.

This is where Blanchot finds himself in 1944. No longer "using Vichy against Vichy,"[31] but not openly active on the side of the Resistance either; wedded to neither the past nor the future considered in their historical reality, but in the aftermath of total disaster, caught at a moment of hiatus in history where literature alone provides the mode in which absolute negativity is the sovereign value. The potential nihilism of his position is clearly evident; to say as he did in 1943 that since Rimbaud literature has been capable of a ruin that renders ruin in the present insignificant aligns him potentially with the worst apologists of the destruction of free peoples.[32] In 1944, the world has caught up with literature: Ruin is total, time is abolished, only an abyssal present endures, and only literature has the measure of the new "human condition" that ruin has brought about. Such an outlook would undeniably be nihilistic if it emanated from a subjectivity that silently held on to its existing form in spite of ruin. Nihilism is always just such a last-ditch ruse. But this is not the case. For Blanchot, like the world, subjectivity too is in ruins. With literature, according to him, this has been the case for some time. Hitherto, the voice of the silent, defunct subject of literature has borrowed the language of existence in the world. Now that alibi has gone, the language of literature is now unmediated, and the writing subject can bear no resemblance to the unitary subject of language. The silence of the writer is thus not merely a refusal to speak. In the literature that takes on form beyond the ruin of everything, no one is there to speak, silence is the silence of writing itself, and writing—*the writing of the disaster*—must forge a discourse and frame a subjectivity commensurate with the new "human condition."

The very last words that Blanchot writes in 1944 point precisely to the threshold at which writing is poised. "Death forevermore Death now" is in itself a purely nihilistic statement, spoken from a position that somehow defies the destruction it denotes. But these words are not Blanchot's: they are a quotation from a poem by Henri Michaux. By thus repeating them, Blanchot maintains the total negation that they signify, while encompassing the "now" to which they refer within another time scale, one in which, by proving repeatable, disaster can be endlessly deferred. "Death now" is no longer the impossible moment that caught the imagination of Jean Paul, Edgar Allan Poe, or Kafka,[33] but the endless recurrence of an end that has really come but can never happen. Sisyphus and Godot will provide emblems of this in the postwar era, but Blanchot has already moved beyond that stage. The form that literature gives to "absolute sovereignty" cannot be a figure. It is a disruptive, "fragmentary" movement that is endlessly in search of itself. Where this movement will lead is clear not even to him in 1944. But within the slim margin of silence separating writing from "death now,"[34] his work will develop over the next half century into new territory for literature, philosophy, and eventually politics, where subjectivity will endlessly go in search of a relation to the Other.

The Mystery of Criticism

There would appear to be nothing very mysterious about criticism. At least, its mystery seems very far removed from the enigma to be found in poetry, for example. At a pinch, were we to wish to grant it a modicum of strangeness, this would be because of its total lack of awareness regarding what it is, what it wants and what it achieves, whereas its origins lie in everything that ought to make the mind clear to itself. That there are a dozen ways of understanding criticism and more than a hundred ways of practicing it is common knowledge, although no one feels inclined to be surprised by it any longer. Ramon Fernandez considers Sainte-Beuve to be the quintessential critic, and in *French Itinerary*,[1] he tries to discover his secret and comes up with definitions of this type: "A critic of Sainte-Beuve's caliber . . . has the gift of being able to translate the vital order into an intellectual one, through the medium of taste and the enjoyment that it provides." Granted, but in that case, if criticism is indeed the ability to recognize living creation and then to transpose it into a set of ideas and images that will make it accessible, what is peculiar is Sainte-Beuve's blindness to creation when it is on the move, when it is happening, when it therefore needs to be recognized: in short, creation that could not be more alive, since it is that of his contemporaries. The fact that Sainte-Beuve recognized neither Baudelaire nor Balzac nor Stendhal—to mention only the Romantics—is an anomaly that can be explained away by his predilection for being unjust or his amorous mishaps. But it is perhaps related to another, better guarded mystery. "If," says Fernandez, "Sainte-Beuve was a great critic in spite of his grudges and in a way in spite of himself, it is no doubt because he knew the secret of criticism." Perhaps this view would need to be completed as follows: If the great critic Sainte-Beuve was unfaithful to such a degree to the central task of criticism, which consists in not calling Baudelaire "abnormal" or Stendhal's *The Charterhouse of Parma* "the work of a wit who tires himself out producing paradoxes," then criticism harbors a secret that is more secret than we care to believe.

Until Jean Paulhan came along, almost no one had noticed this. But from *The Flowers of Tarbes* to the essay on Félix Fénéon (which recently appeared in *Confluences*),[2] he teaches us to circumscribe and indeed understand a mystery that places criticism further from our reach than either poetry or the novel. To begin with, there can be no certainty that criticism exists. Not even the nineteenth century, which was known as the century of criticism, or even the twentieth, when the greatest writers have turned their art into a critical reflection on art, ever convincingly produced an individual who could represent criticism the way Mallarmé or Rimbaud represent poetry. Why is that? It is tempting to think that we have no way of knowing. Is it because the minds that seize hold of literary works in order to judge them are too dissimilar? Or remote from each other? Or too confident despite their uncertainty, or too lax despite their rigor? Is it because they eventually get things wrong? This is often manifestly the case, and it makes the critic's condition rather a thankless one: It is never possible to say (or prove) that a poet is wrong, but a Sainte-Beuve figure does get it wrong; he falls within the category of error; he himself provides the evidence to suggest that that he is not what he seeks to be. In a hundred years Jean Paulhan can find only one man who was capable of preferring Rimbaud, Mallarmé, Lautréamont, and Charles Cros above all others and of recognizing Gide, Proust, Valéry, and Claudel before anyone else. Even then, this rarest of critics, whom one might even call unique, this Félix Fénéon almost declined to be a writer, as if the critic's true nature obliged him to become invisible, to make himself scarce, not to exist.

Literature is quite often considered a form of sacrifice. "You sacrifice the possessions that you abuse."[3] For example, a lamb is offered up in mitigation for the abuse, whether mercantile or alimentary, of the flock as a whole; the reality from which we seek to derive limitless enjoyment is subjected to a limited amount of destruction that the ritual act endows with supreme value. Literature, and specifically poetry, can be seen as the sacrifice of language: It is or has the intention of being the immolation of discourse, its destruction; it seeks to ruin words that are designed for practical use and make them unusable. In literature, language is the victim, and the hope of the writer like the belief of the sacrificant is that, at the moment of its destruction, the sacrificed object, be it a word or an animal, will become sacred; what disappears acquires supreme value, destroys the specific features that define it and becomes a figure for absolute sovereignty. This perhaps explains the ambiguous attitude that people find surprising in writers. They mistreat words and bring about their destruction, and yet through this holocaust they believe they are restoring inestimable value to words; their sole purpose seems to be the total destruction of language, yet they appear to have only one goal in mind: to restore its true nature to language, to make it exist. On the sacrificial pyre, the substitution of the ram for Isaac does not just signify the right to live that has been restored to the man who has risked or offered his life, but also, as the prefiguration of the lamb who will become God, it declares that the sacrificial act has transformed the victim, and that in place of the ordinary individual it has brought forth the sacred.

What is a critic? A poet, but one who approaches poetry by way of nonbeing, in that he does not wish to be a poet; a novelist who is privy to the secret of novel creation and yet says no to the novel. Is he then the specialist who refuses to be a specialist in any particular genre, and who, ranging from the play to the essay, knows everything, judges everything and is everything? This has been argued, but no doubt wrongly so on that count. For the true critic, who is already a poet without being a poet, and a novelist without writing novels, also has the ambition not to be that specialist in nonspecialization we call a critic. Being inside poetry and yet outside it too, he wishes to remain outside criticism, and if possible, to practice it by means of silence, or else in such a way that by writing he appears above all as someone who does not write. This is admittedly a desperate ambition. But there is nothing to say that it is not richly significant. If the writer who is concerned at the dangers of writing is the sacrificant who protests against the abuse of words in practical language by condemning words to a destruction that is a revelation; if the poet will not rest until he has denounced himself for being a poet, if he considers himself first and foremost as suspect, feeling only anguish and fear at the assurance that the easy brilliance of language provides, it would be quite surprising if the critic alone could enjoy being a literary practitioner in tranquility, comprehend and range over all of literature without any shame for what he is doing, or without the constant urge to be put inconspicuously to death. Clearly, only scorn is reserved for criticism that is not its own contestation, but the tranquil exercise of a vain and presumptuous power. In the past, during popular festivities, kings and chiefs were sometimes sacrificed in effigy in order to redeem, at least through an ideal (and sometimes bloody) sacrifice, the abuse that all sovereignty represents. The traditional critic is a sovereign who eludes immolation, assumes he can exercise authority without expiating it and wishes to be the master of a kingdom that he possesses without risk. There is consequently no more wretched a sovereign, nor one who, for having refused to be anything at all, could come closer to being nothing.

—January 6, 1944

dogmatic content of faith. What can be the meaning of such an attitude? It is not without its ambiguities. First of all, the Hindu syncretism that allows Christ to figure in Ramakrishna's visions naturally extends the same privilege to Mohammed or Buddha. The unity of truth means that no participation is excluded. This benevolent attitude toward particular beliefs drains them of all reality, and by depriving them of what they are, raises them to a universal level. Lanza del Vasto reports a discussion he had with in fact rather an unfaithful disciple of Adi Shankara, the master of the Vedanta. After making a Christian profession of faith of the purest kind, this philosopher said: "I confess that Jesus Christ is the Son of the living God, a true man and a true god . . . etc.," before adding rather angrily, as if someone had contradicted him: "And why, pray, could the Almighty not put on flesh?" "I waited open-mouthed for what he would say next," says Lanza del Vasto, "and what came next was this: 'He has done it so many times.'"

But this ambiguity is too visible to be dangerous. There is, however, another more serious one. By turning toward the West, and making itself comprehensible by borrowing its concepts, methods, and myths, it is likely that Hinduism has deprived outsiders of any hope of ever penetrating its secrets, and through appearing very close to them, it has become infinitely remote. What do modern-day Hindus see in these overtures whereby they appear to place their morality or their contemplation within our reach? Probably no more than a polite gesture, an act of intellectual courtesy that obliges them to explain themselves in European terms, and momentarily to adopt our ways of seeing and judging (but precisely because these concessions are of no importance in themselves, and leave aside what is essential). As a result, Westerners feel that they do not need to make much of an effort to understand the wisdom that has been brought down to their level, and henceforth they are all the more estranged from it for no longer having a sense of what makes it strange, and for believing that they have access, intellectually at least, to a spiritual discipline without being aware of everything that separates them from it. This vulgarization has naturally encouraged misunderstandings, but it is the most serious and significant of the Hindu books that bear the primary responsibility for creating the facile perspectives that make Hinduism appear definitively contaminated by the West.

The case of Gandhi is significant in this regard. There is no reason to judge the Mahatma, either for what he is or for what he represents according to Hindu tradition. But from outside, he looks like the man who is least equipped to introduce Western minds to the spiritual ideal of his country, precisely because he seems to have adapted it to fit our ambitions. Lanza del Vasto emphasizes the "modern" features of the man he reveals to us. It is the spirit of Christianity that awakened the ancestral virtues in him. Tolstoy's evangelical musings provided the initial impact. Reading the Gospels confirmed his choice of path; he even considered becoming a Christian. What is more, a Westerner can see himself mirrored in him: His readiness to act, his sense of historical opportunity, and his organizational powers are entirely Western qualities. Far from belittling action, he is the first Hindu to make it the goal of his teaching and to give social and national significance to a purely inner discipline. Naturally, as we are all aware, Gandhi's politics do not aim solely for a political victory but for a spiritual victory too: He wants to free the people of their ills and their ignorance, to let them live the truth. All that is entirely clear. What is also clear is that among those ills, there is first and foremost the presence of the foreigner, and that the system promoted by the Mahatma, and in whose service he enlists the forces of spirituality, is a system of political, economic and social liberation. It is impossible not to see in this rehabilitation of external action a distortion of the spiritual ideal. Man is no longer required to strip himself bare for nothing (with no coherent goal to justify this total annihilation); he is called on to organize the world, to overcome himself in order to make reality better. This is an ignominious return to the most vulgar doctrine of salvation. As for the celebrated method of nonviolence—which undoubtedly has its own nobility and worth—Lanza del Vasto acknowledges that the Hindu leaders have recourse to it not for the religion signification it possesses, but because of its efficacy, "because it delivers the goods." Such is the dominion or the morality of action. There are no higher values that it does not reduce to its own means, authorizing them only to the extent that they serve a purpose and "deliver the goods."

—January 13, 1944

From One Novel to Another

It is generally agreed that in a novel, the subject counts for very little—especially if what is understood by subject is a story that can be summarized or retold, and through which the anecdotal significance of the book is conveyed. The subject is not confined to the plot: It depends just as much on verbal episodes, on compositional detail, and even more so on the images that reveal the meaning of what has been created. The subject of a novel is first and foremost the world it brings into being. Nonetheless, the choice of anecdote also deserves to be looked at in passing, because it is often strange and is one of the things by which a book may be judged. For example, why did Christian Megret, a skilled and congenial novelist, decide, in *In Those Days*, to tell us the story of Stephanas the potter, a Christian from Asia Minor who survived persecution only to lapse into heresy?[1] Was he tempted by the historical depiction of the early Church? But he has little time for erudition, and it would be surprising if a writer were to try to rewrite the adventure of *Quo Vadis* or *Sanguis martyrum*.[2] Was the only reason he described the end of a world so as to find in it a reflection of our own turmoil? But Megret pays little heed to the pure demands of history, and he is very careful not to intermingle images of a former age with the spirit of our own in a facile way. Was it then the psychological case of this Christian, guilty of being too rigorous and unrelentingly pious, that appeared "modern" to him, and worthy of prolonged study? That may well be the case, but because we do not always share the author's interest for his hero, the book remains an enigma, and the attention we give it is focused on a virtuoso performance whose meaning is impenetrable. What is certain is that the novelist has sought to give his portrait an air of truthfulness and life. All of the set pieces we can expect in a book like this, from circus games and combats with lions to scenes of debauchery in the governor's palace, reveal those picturesque, zestful, and natural qualities that are the sign of a writer's skill. But where is the truth in all of that? It is, precisely, nothing more than surface appearance.

A reproach that can be leveled at Louis Parrot's novel *Salt Store* is that its choice of subject is strangely unclear.[3] Sometimes the book seems like the story of a young man from the provinces who, having set off to make his fortune, experiences his own inadequacy, then returns to his roots and resigns himself to a wretched life. At others, the novel is about the salt store and its rich owner, a foundling who has become one of the richest industrialists in Touraine and lords it over the entire region, imposing his ways and ignoring custom before finally falling victim to his own dreams. Or else the novelist turns his attention to the town itself and its inhabitants, and to life in the provinces, and he describes these with such a profound feeling for their secrets that he appears to abandon all other perspectives, so that the subject of his novel is now just the setting in which the story develops. The outcome is a nebulous composition that leaves the mind of the sort of reader who prefers things to have a clear order, with the feeling that there is something unbalanced about it, something that he has qualms about accepting. But of what value are objections like this? In our view, they neglect the true meaning of the work. If we are initially surprised by the disconnectedness and the tentative alternation of superimposed plotlines, we soon realize that they are organized at a deeper level, and we yield to the entanglements of the story as it develops its figures and its intentions on several levels. The novelist has visibly sought to write a sort novel of the quagmire. This quagmire is in some sense physical, even geographical. The subject is the silting up of the Loire, whose streams of earth arrest and stem its flow, turning the river into a "badly painted mirror." The powerful industrialist from Touraine has waged a futile struggle to prevent the river from silting up; but his stubborn efforts have been powerless to overcome the obstacles, and his success is finally compromised by the disappointment of ultimate defeat. The quagmire is a threat to each of the characters. It rules the town, and the young man whose dismal amorous adventures are described to us, appears in his turn to be another victim of the same fatal inertia. If Louis Parrot had merely brought together the story of the river and that of his characters through a play on words, the symbol would be unbearably artificial, and the novel would collapse beneath the weight of its own vacuity. But his achievement on the contrary has been to provide a physical image of the quagmire. The descriptions of the Lower Loire region, of the town that the river engulfs in its laziness, of the presence of this dark, sluggish river that comes to life at night and whose alluvial lethargy can never be alleviated, make the lives of its inhabitants comprehensible to us. Here, destiny takes the form of flood of sand against which no one could conceivably swim. The most serious criticism that can be leveled at this often remarkable first novel concerns the moral, optimistic outcome that the novelist has seen fit to invent for it. Since young Cholaine is strictly speaking neither feeble nor mediocre, but simply the prisoner of an incurable torpor, why does he suddenly wake up? Why does the debauchery he did not object to until then suddenly appear impossible and blameworthy? The entire development of the book jars with this conclusion. It is false and disagreeable, and it casts doubt on the authenticity of a book that ends up saying the opposite of what it means to say.

A writer who writes a first novel is tempted to borrow his "subject" from his solitary childhood or from events in the family. That is what Raoul Dujardin has done in *The Well-Behaved Child* and Jean Milo in *Family Feeling*.[4] The resemblance between these two novels goes no further than the subject they have in common. In other words, they are almost entirely different. There is no better proof of how little weight the story that defines it carries in a novel. *The Well-Behaved Child*, with its scenes of war, the distress of a child who must live far away from his mother because his mother lives with soldiers whom she picks up, and last the anxieties of an adolescence that shyness locks away inside itself, could have been one of those cruel books in which delicate impressions are no more than a deceptive background against which the sad realities of the early years are drawn. *Family Feeling*, by contrast, which describes a bourgeois family where everyone leads a mediocre but peaceful life, gives happiness and tender dreams their chance. Each of the authors has turned away from the direction in which their novel was tending. The cruel novel becomes a tender, delicate book where great sorrows are dispelled and small pleasures endure; and the family portrait becomes a harsh caricature that ends with a crime. Dujardin's novel is rather thin; it is made up of a series of short chapters, written simply, and it leaves an impression of ease and candor. Jean Milo's book is rather copious, detail is piled on detail and the effects are repeated without becoming more intense. Milo describes a character who is pretentious and obsessive, who reduces his entire family to poverty and ends up an idiot. Facing him, he portrays a young boy who is tender and stubborn, and who struggles gently and reasonably against this mean and petty life and finally escapes from it, promising himself that he will never impose the seal of marriage and the forms of family life on the love that he eventually finds. All this is unaffected, free of ostentation and perfectly agreeable. There is something limpid about this murky story in which we glimpse a sort of grace.

—January 20, 1944

The Four Gospels

Hubert Pernot is no orthodox critic, but nor is he a purely negative one, and his work will be of considerable interest even to those who are unwilling to cast doubt on the dogmatic value of the Gospels. The translation of the Gospels that he has just published is merely a part of a larger undertaking.[1] It follows studies of the language and the original text of the Gospels, and it should be followed by another translation, designed to shed further light on the version that can be considered the best there is today.

Hubert Pernot's viewpoint is as follows: One of the faults of biblical criticism lies in its neglect of many of the Greek manuscripts, or of those manuscripts partially translated from Greek and which, in the absence of the originals, provide points of reference for traditional scholarship. Though these manuscripts have been catalogued and described, most of them remain unknown. Others that have been published display variants to which comparative studies are only just beginning to draw attention. It is far from certain therefore whether the currently accepted text—the received text—can be considered definitive. It is not always based on the best manuscripts or the most ancient ones. Established as it was in order to give stability to a tradition whose unity risked being compromised from the outset by too many separate versions, it reflects a codification that was more or less complete by the fourth century.

Pernot's critical approach is two-pronged: It disputes the choice of manuscripts on which today's translations are based, but it considers it possible to establish a purer text, one that is less laden with obscurities and more coherent. Generally speaking, he finds that people have resigned themselves too easily to attributing to the evangelist unsatisfactory passages that only skillful translation prevents from arousing misgivings in the reader. The adapters often leave a visible trace; what were mostly late revisions have encouraged the harmonization of the different Gospels at the expense of their internal unity. Pernot even goes so far as to claim that a reader who, out of fidelity to the overall tone, were to eliminate the dissonances and take no account of the manuscript tradition, would end up with a better text than the one found in today's editions. These remarks are by no means entirely new. Orthodox critics such as Father Lagrange have themselves admitted that it is better in many cases to seek an overall concordance, rather than aim for a strict harmonization that would threaten the stability of each version.[2] Furthermore, Pernot's views are as yet still a matter of conjecture, presented in notes and often concerning points of detail. It is thus only possible to assess their tendencies, not to judge their results.

The most interesting hypotheses concern the Gospel according to Saint John. According to Pernot, this Gospel is made up of disparate elements. In its first, shorter version, which is predominantly narrative in nature and familiar in tone, although symbolic in what it expresses, it represents a more ancient tradition (when we are aware of it) than that of the synoptic Gospels. However, it quite quickly became a liturgy. The narrative parts were read out loud, and officiants divided into separate groups would intone some of its sequences, repeating passages that voices echoed back to each other, binding responses into the fabric of the recitative, repeating the finals at the beginning of the versicles. This explains the numerous repetitions designed to maintain the rhythm or allow one officiant to take over from the other. This hypothesis is by no means a revolutionary one. It merely extends to the fourth Gospel as a whole an explanation that people have long been tempted to apply to the prologue, which is manifestly composed in a rhythm that is based on alternating voices and the use of a certain sort of intoning. Indeed Father Jousse has defended a quite similar theory to Pernot's concerning the origin of the Gospel texts, though Pernot's version is less adventurous and more attentive to the facts.[3] After many others, Pernot emphasizes the symbolic nature of the principal episodes. Jesus the light giving sight to the blind, Jesus the life feeding the five thousand, the encounter with the Samaritan woman (whose five husbands can be seen as the five gods introduced into the land by foreign peoples, the sixth—who is not her husband—being the God of Israel), the miraculous draught of fishes during the fourth appearance, or else the active parables constituted by certain miracles (such as the cursing of the fig tree) all have an allegorical value that no commentator would question. But does the symbol exhaust the reality of the story? That is something that criticism is powerless to argue.

Pernot's translation satisfies two goals. Remaining close to the received text, which is precisely the one whose purity he disputes, its precision tends to highlight the flaws in that version; instead of concealing the doubtful passages through expressive finesse or invisible adjustments, it offers us the current version with its rambling and its occasional contradictions. But in addition, Pernot has sought to render the style more faithfully. The language of the Gospels is still a living language. As he puts it, today it is more easily understandable to a Greek than Montaigne's language is to a Frenchman. The evangelists were addressing the people; they were not concerned with bookish turns of phrase, but used the spoken tongue, which is very close to what is still spoken today. The language of Mark is everyday Greek. In some parts, that of John is no less familiar, though it contains some peculiarities of dialect. "Matthew achieves a happy medium." Only Luke writes in a more learned sort of Greek, because his education probably made him shun the style of everyday speech. This new translation therefore aims to strip the French of the Gospels of its borrowed graces, and it attempts to convey to today's reader the same impression that Greek may have had on audiences in the early centuries. This produces innovations of various sorts. Pernot notes, for example, that the word Christ has become a proper name, and so has lost its meaning as Messiah. In his translation Christ becomes the Anointed; similarly, in order for the meaning of his title to be restored, John the Baptist becomes John the Immersionist. Simon is not called Peter, but Rock (which corresponds more closely to the Aramaic and Hebrew term). Publicans are customs officials (*gabelous*). When necessary, the translator calls on popular expressions; surprised to hear Christ teaching with such authority in the temple, his fellow countrymen say: "Wherever did he pick that up?" ("Where then did this man get all these things?" is Father Crampon's translation).[4] Elsewhere, the Jews who wonder about Jesus's mission no longer use the traditional words "How long will you keep us in suspense?" (John 10:24), but instead, "How much longer are you going to go on boring us?" And Christ himself, using a popular turn of phrase, says to his listeners, "You are born of the Devil's father" and not "You are of your father the devil" (John 8:44). It should be noted too that in the Lord's Prayer, the translator replaces Jerome's text, which in fact the latter proposed only tentatively, with the following: "Give us our bread of tomorrow today," which becomes in Luke: "Give us each day our daily bread" (Luke 11:2).

A language that we translate often appears to contain more imagery, and be more concrete than our own; where the translator discovers an image, in the original language there is sometimes merely a cliché that is invisible and without metaphorical significance. In the same way, a translation that seeks both textual precision and expressive accuracy can encounter difficult problems. Studying the various meanings of the word "*psuche*," Pernot decides to translate it by the word "being" and not by the word "life" or "soul": "Do not worry about your being (Luke 12:22) . . . whoever seeks to keep his being will lose it" (Luke 17: 33). Or else, considering that the Greek word "*pistis*" has a broader meaning than our word "faith," and implies a notion of confidence, he regularly uses the word "fidence" [*fiance*]: "I say to you, not even in Israel have I found such great fidence" (Luke 7:9). But the word "being" is anomalous and the word "fidence" is an archaism. Consequently, neither corresponds to current French usage, and so they inevitably betray the form of the Greek text by their contrived appearance. Thus it is that precision can give rise to error, and as Paul Mazon says of the language of Homer,[5] to translate concrete detail scrupulously is to distort what is natural about the original movement of the text.

—January 27, 1944

From Jean-Paul to Giraudoux

It would perhaps be an exaggeration to claim that Jean-Paul has had any particular influence on contemporary literature, and yet the great German Romantic not only followed the same path as some of the writers of our own time, but in addition, his metaphorical style aligns him so closely with one of our finest writers, Jean Giraudoux, that he seems like his impassioned double. What lies behind these similarities? They are always very mysterious. Jean-Paul, who was little known in France and indeed little known in Germany, was revealed to our literary world by Mme de Staël; the "Speech of the Dead Christ," an anguished dream before the emptiness of heaven, created a great stir, and Nerval presented the same vision in his "Christ on the Mount of Olives." For a century, that was about all. Philarète Chasles's translation of *Titan* remained unread, and even in Germany, this writer, once as famous as Goethe, was entirely forgotten. It took Stefan George's anthology to bring back to light someone who from now on will be known as "the Jean-Paul of harmony and dream." During the last twenty years he has not been without friends in France. One of the most faithful of these, Edmond Jaloux, and one of the most active, Albert Béguin, have between them done a great deal to reveal the poet's true nature to us. Béguin devoted a chapter of *The Romantic Soul and the Dream* to him, and he has translated *Hesperus*, *The Jubilee*, and a selection of dreams that make up an infinitely precious volume. Today, Pierre Velut has pursued these efforts by publishing a complete version of *Quintus Fixlein*.[1]

At the dawn of Romanticism, Jean-Paul stood for a number of assumptions whose value escaped the French Romantics, but that, either after them or alongside them, had a profound effect on our times. The main one consists of an acknowledgment that literature is by nature an experience; it has become an expression of spirituality; it initiates whoever pursues it into a new mode of existence; it is a sort of asceticism that allows us to progress toward a more authentic life. In a word, it has a mystical significance for the writer. (Later, a century later, another writer in German, Kafka, will say: To write is to pray.) Whereas for most Romantics, art is subjective because it reveals the inner movements and expresses the personal intimacy of the writer, for the Romanticism or the pre-Romanticism of Hölderlin, Jean-Paul, or Novalis, as well as for Nerval or Rimbaud, art is subjective because it concerns what is most profound in an artist and aims not simply to express it but to transform it. For our Romantics, art retains a psychological value. It is a sincere expression, a faithful mirroring; for foreign Romantics, the value of literature is that it engages the writer: It does not express, it unsettles. It is both a means of knowing and a power of metamorphosis; living and writing are a single act. Poetry is a magical experience.

Jean-Paul discovered his poetic talent relatively late, and in remarkable circumstances: The son of a poor family, so poor that his younger brother drowned himself to relieve his family of the burden of feeding him; having lost not only this brother but the only two friends to whom he felt able to talk, overwhelmed by poverty and misery, one night he experienced the revelation of his death, he saw himself dead, he really took the form of a corpse. "That evening," he noted later, "I found my way to my own deathbed, across a span of thirty years I saw myself with the drooping hand of a corpse, the wasted face of a sick man, a glazed eye, and I heard the delirious ravings that I will utter on my last night" (and indeed he did die on the anniversary of his vision, thirty-five years later). "You will surely come, o supreme dream, and since that is a certainty . . . I take my leave today of both the earth and its sky." This revelation stems from both his intellect and his imagination, and it plunges him into a state of extraordinary creative frenzy; abandoning the arid satirical literature to which he had so far applied himself unsuccessfully, he shatters the humdrum outer shell of reality and discovers beneath the formlessness of things a wellspring, a scintillation of images, an infinite life that his art, heady and obsessed with comparisons, allows him to grasp hold of. Henceforth, his work develops in two directions. Sometimes, rising above the level of everyday life, he describes the magnificent sanctuaries, aglow with the light of dreams, toward which those "fine souls," those "higher men" who cannot easily tolerate the pettiness of social life are drawn. At others, he returns to the humblest forms of existence and turns his attention to simple souls, to pastors, schoolmasters, and schoolboys, and in their modest quirks he finds, rather as Dickens does, a reflection of the pure, limitless life that his yearning for transfiguration seeks everywhere in nature. It is to this idyllic, naïve vein that *Quintus Fixlein*, translated by Pierre Velut, belongs.

The singular nature of Jean-Paul's art stems from the role that it gives to image. There is no writer for whom writing is, to such a degree, the power to metamorphose things through the invention of metaphors. For him, comparisons are not just figures that display a superficial stylistic interest; they are also a path of discovery, a track that leads us by degrees from the visible to the invisible, from the known to the unknown, from the familiar to the self-evidence of enigma. That is an aspect of art that has nowadays become very common. But Jean-Paul was one of the first novelists to sense that metaphor could be an extraordinary instrument of transformation, and gripped by a veritable frenzy, his prose exchanges everything for everything, assembles the strangest of harmonies, produces the most fantastical of coincidences, and recreates the world by making it the site of a universal resemblance. This ability to advance by means of digression, this gift for expressing the same with what is other makes him not just "the father of contemporary expressionism," as Stefan George claims, but also the precursor of a writer as original and as free of influences as Giraudoux. An interesting study could be made of these two writers. Both of them are in search of those "great resemblances" that "leave a gash on the world and here and there mark it with light," in the knowledge that "out of them all nostalgia, all spirit, all emotion can be born."[2] Both writers not only take hold of things and objects so as to transform them into images; they also use literary images, allusions to books, art, and the world of culture as material for other images or for actual objects. Each of them indulges in an outpouring of erudition that, in the German poet, can sometimes develop into tiresome pedantry. Finally, both of them wish to rediscover what is innocent and authentic about the world, what gives it its grace and makes us the contemporaries of its original purity, of a truth which is that of the first act, of the first steps, of everything that is a birth and a beginning. Alongside these common features there would of course be many differences to observe. The first one seems to us to relate to the movement of images that, in Jean-Paul, develop haphazardly, in an intoxicated outpouring that is powerfully incoherent; Jean Giraudoux, on the other hand creates an attraction between each image, links them each to the other through a dialectical progression in which they gradually go from day to night, before finally exploding in the heart of darkness with the memory of what once was the most brilliant light. But let us reread these sentences: "Now, with each star that disappeared in the firmament above, a flower and a bird awoke down here on earth."—"He had appeared in the fog, like spring or a

Homeric god."—"His childhood friend disappeared from his sight like childhood." Taken from *Hesperus* and previously cited opportunely by Albert Béguin, they give an idea of the secret affinity that can unite two writers, and of how metaphor can join together across time the greatest flights of poetry.

—February 3, 1944

A Diary without Episodes

Three years ago, Raymond Dumay published his first novel, a simple, gentle book that was full of grace, in which he portrayed a group of shepherds living on the banks of the Saône.[1] Today he has published his war diary and a collection of novellas, *My Calmest Face* and *Springtime of Men*.[2] Both of these books have the same simplicity and the same freshness. Perhaps their reader may occasionally feel that the ease has become more studied, the candor more self-conscious, but their charm is just as pure, and we read with such harmonious pleasure that our impression is that such harmony is not the work of chance, and that this young author knows what he wants and is going where it suits him to go.

Raymond Dumay has deliberately left the war out of his war diary. "Those who read this diary will be surprised to find so many 'blanks,' corresponding precisely to everything that could bear any relation to the war. The 'blanks' correspond to the invasion of France, to the silence of my friends who are at the front, and to my love." Such discretion is certainly appealing. It surrounds his slim volume with an aura of silence that transforms the words a little, endowing the gentlest of them with a dullness, a shadowy resonance that the ear can discern. For the same reasons, the first pages, which express the horror of war, are not the best. It is not enough for a feeling to be accurate; the way it is expressed must also make it totally specific and individual, link it to a single soul, and restore for us what is general about it through what makes its development unique. The nostalgia for peace becomes a sort of sullenness for Raymond Dumay, a peevish indignation that argues without rhyme or reason and that he himself will eventually pour scorn on. Nonetheless, there is nothing inflated about his anger or any false piety in his disapproval: We are struck above all by the reactions of a mind that avoids vulgar complacency and finds nobility in simplicity.

Facts count for nothing in this diary without episodes. The author spent three months in Saint-Maxent, then, once he had received his commission, he was posted to Maisons-Laffitte; later on he went to La Ferté-sous-Jouarre, where his job was to look after his platoon. He moved on to the north, and then came the retreat—but between June 7 and June 25 the diary is silent, as though the vanished memories of those days could tolerate neither the precision nor the truth that characterize language. So what happened during that war for the young writer? Nothing and everything. Born in Bresse, and having spent his adolescence as a shepherd who was no different from any other country boy, his origins have left him with a love for things, a liking for what is familiar and clear about life that transfigures everything he encounters. Each stage of his war becomes an arranged meeting with a season, a bird, or a simple soul. Saint-Maxent sees him visit the honey seller who, ensconced in dingy shop, tells him of a field of buckwheat in bloom, or a great lime tree filled with bees, and who, miserly though she be, hands him a pot of her finest pale honey. When he is billeted in La Ferté, he encounters a pure and gentle countryside where blackbirds, wood pigeons, and bullfinches luxuriate in the spring. "Here in the midst of the tart plum tree flowers a young finch, entirely gray as well as totally modest, rolls and unrolls its tongue in trills that gush forth like drops of water, and diving over my awning, its female leaps onto its neck, teasing him till they both fall, wings and legs entwined, in a shower of petals." Even the darkest days have moments when they are lit up by dream: At dawn, the dark village of June 7 becomes a village made of crystal; the fountains play, water flows from the walls, the trees disown the dirty houses. "In front of the barn I stopped to listen to some finches singing; I went in and saw them; there were three of them outlined against a windowpane set into the roof."

Some may find that there is a scandalous air of happiness about this book. How, during such tragic moments, in periods of such great anguish, can anyone sustain this impression of happiness, this appetite for life, for writing, for spontaneously gathering gentle images, for being constantly in tune with the world thanks to such preposterous grace? But what makes this little book authentic is precisely the fact that this joy always appears unsullied. Throughout the hours of distress it never grows dim, but never alters them either; discouragement has its own special gaiety, just as unhappiness has its own smile, and this gratuitous levity is created by someone who has enough affection and enough indifference to be able to love life in all its horror, and accept it in all its evil. Moreover, this sense of happiness is not just an innocent instinct, one that is unaware of what it is seeking and was not expecting what it finds. Raymond Dumay speaks simply of it as an art to which he has devoted his life: "I have often professed myself a happy man, and I feel neither shame nor regret for doing so . . . I believe that happiness is a lengthy apprenticeship, and if I am so perfectly happy at present, it is because for a long time I was unhappy." These are words in which there is no enigma, and yet they have the gentle power of a perfect secret.

The entire diary is written in a very simple language that sometimes sings a little, or decks itself out with delicate images, as if to reveal beneath the veil of a chosen color the naked beauty of a word. Raymond Dumay is not afraid to make use of clichés. He sings their praises, sees them as a pathway to poetry, gives them a new youth, his own, and if he writes, "When I return home, a nightingale is singing in the darkness," it is as if we are hearing the nightingale for the first time, as if henceforth, thanks to him, its song is that of the confidence and the beauty of night. In fact, what stands out in this style is a certain accent, a quality of expression belonging to a soul that is without flaw. What he says is not exceptional; his way of saying it is even simpler, but this transparency and lightness, wreathed in a quizzical smile, is the promise of an alliance, an alliance with the world of reconciliation. Perhaps one ought to inquire why Raymond Dumay is much less successful and adept in his novellas than he is in his diary. They are of good quality, but often rather empty. He is not suited to storytelling; the tale becomes overburdened with episodes, can never quite find a plot, and survives only through unconnected details and images. One of the merits of *The Grass Is Growing in the Meadow* lies in its indifference to the story that it lazily allows to develop. The novellas in *Springtime of Men* are more serious. They have a beginning and an end, and when they are finished, they disappoint us because they link depictions that we find charming with facts that never succeed in interesting us. What do we ask of a writer who has such a happy talent for simplicity and ease? That he spare us any artificial invention and offer us his discoveries directly, with the ease and purity that make *My Calmest Face* a pale replica of Jean Giraudoux's *Adorable Clio* and make it worthy of the same epigraph: "Forgive me o war for—at every opportunity—having caressed you."[3]

—February 10, 1944

On the Subject of Language

Albert Dauzet's excellent book on the subject of *Linguistic Geography* allows us to see the illusions that have affected science whenever it has been applied to language.[1] Taking as its subject a relatively recent discipline founded by Jules Gilliéron and developed by various scientists from France and elsewhere, this book studies the way in which the most thorough research into popular modes of speaking has transformed the science of language.[2] The first linguists to study patois readily believed that they were in touch with the living reality of language. They demolished the rigidities of the framework of laws that the neogrammarians had proudly established by starting with existing words and going back to their prototypes. They followed words not only from province to province but also from village to village and family to family. Noting the importance of exceptions, they came to the conclusion that it was not each language or even each dialect that had its own history and its particular way of conforming to laws, but rather each word taken and situated in its concrete existence. In short, the ambition of the new linguists led them to replace logical constructions that were too pure with the much more variegated reality of language. Not language as "it" is spoken in general, but as this person or that person speaks it, in the infinite diversity of its developments.

This ideal very quickly turned out to be fanciful. Where is concrete reality to be found? Is it in literary language, or everyday language, or argot? Or does it not lie rather in the depths of an individual's consciousness? Psychologists have long been aware that the word—be it the abstract word found in the dictionary or the private word with its own resonances—is not what is truly real about language: The concrete structure is provided by the sentence, which is a force field, a mold waiting to be filled, a direction and a signifying perspective. But there is a still a distinction to be made. Considered as a living reality, the sentence is not the one we hear or the one that is garnered from questionnaires and that is given once and for all; it is solely in the consciousness of the person who expresses it that it acquires concrete value, because it is thereby turned into an act; someone makes it their own, takes responsibility for it, and is free to arrange it in order to achieve self-expression. As Jean-Paul Sartre has very clearly shown, language is not a language that speaks by itself.[3] In speech, in order to find reality, you have to go back to the speaker.

Albert Dauzet does not reveal all of the difficulties encountered by the new linguistics, but he very judiciously sets out its limitations, and ultimately reconciles it with the science of the neogrammarians. They were rather too eager to confine the way in which words evolve within grammatical categories; today it is clearer that linguistic forms have links with the soil, that the battles they wage are not concerned with entirely abstract provinces but with well-defined geographical regions. Their journeys and their migration can be followed on a map; the great highways that they travel can be uncovered; the reasons for their decline and their death can be understood. But all of these more minute descriptions pose no threat to the laws established by the classical school; indeed they respect them, because at the heart of the language to which they are applied there is always an abstract language, something that is a given and that remains general enough to become an object for science. Within these limits there is nothing more fascinating than the strange existence of words, their obstinacy, their weakness and the struggles during which a given word attacks a given form, overcomes it, feeds on it, and through its victory gradually acquires a different meaning. For example, linguistic geography studies the collision of homonyms. What happens when phonological developments make two words with different meanings converge on the same figure? One of them eliminates the other, obliging it to find itself another form through either borrowing or metaphor. Hence, if argot calls work *le boulot*, it will not use the verb *boulotter* to mean "to work," because the verb already means "to eat" and so is not available; therefore, using another word that is as close as possible to it, *boulon*, to which it attaches the meaning of *boulot*—it creates the verb *boulonner*, and that way, telescoping is avoided. By contrast, if regular phonetic development causes two terms to converge without coinciding, a phenomenon of attraction occurs, and the more powerful word deflects the weaker word from its path. What is the origin of the popular expression *tomber dans les pommes*, fall into a faint (*tomber en pâmoison*)? It is the word *pâme*, which is a verbal noun derived from *pâmer*, to swoon (hence *tomber dans les pâmes*), that has been attracted by the common word *pomme*, apple, and has yielded to it, even though no semantic amphibology can result from this encounter.

Words travel along the normal routes of invasion and trade. Our main artery is the great valley of the Saône and the Rhône. As soon as a word enters this corridor, according to Gilliéron, it will unfailingly follow it down south to the sea; it is by this route that northern France has drawn on the France of the Midi, and by the same route, Parisian neologisms have descended as far as the Mediterranean; by contrast, old words endure in the east, the west, the Alps, and in the Massif Central. The expression *compère-loriot* arose in the vicinity of Malmédy. The initial moment of its birth was the confusing of *l'orgéol*, a little grain of barley (*l'orge*), with *l'oriol*, the name of a bird, the oriole. But why *compère*, godfather, or more usually, accomplice? Because in Walloon a distinction exists between *merle noir* (blackbird) and *merle oriol* (oriole), which became *merloriol*. This word rapidly changed in peasant language to become *mère-loriot* (mother *loriot*), which gave rise to *père-loriot* (father *loriot*); *compère* inevitably followed. Leaving Malmédy, the expression reached Burgundy, where you find *fils-loriot* and *filles-loriot* (son *loriot* and daughter *loriot*), before heading for Provence, where nowadays *fils-loriot* has become *figue-loriot* (fig *loriot*).

Far from disparaging the reforming efforts of the old grammarians or the work of rectification and conservation that literary works carry out, Dauzet approves of them in principle and considers them of service to the life of a language. That is one of the most remarkable lessons of his book. Not so long ago, it was still accepted that the idioms of primitive peoples and the different patois were the only pure languages, governed by natural forces alone, whereas literary languages, improved by grammarians, displayed worrying symptoms of sclerosis and were no longer anything but artificial constructs, devoid of life. A more serious study of dialects came to an entirely different conclusion. It was observed that all language, left to itself, declines under the influence of the laws of phonetics and the effect of homonyms; sometimes language tries to defend itself when it feels threatened. It applies "therapeutic poultices" to itself, but these expedients are insufficient, and to make up for its losses it needs a scientific language to place a limit on its excesses. According to Gilliéron, if the French spoken in Paris had experienced the phenomena that affected various northern patois without reacting, the Latin sentence "*Merula amat mel apium in apiaro*" (the blackbird likes the honey of the bees in the hive, *la merle aime le miel des abeilles dans la ruche*) would have resulted in this extraordinary amalgam of ambiguity and solecism: "the black mother has dear the tear of the wasps in the fly" (*la noire mère a cher la larme des guèpes dans la mouche*). The main instrument of salvation for our language has been the restoration of its links with Latin; it was this reference to a solid language that, particularly during the Renaissance, put a stop to the destructive action of phonetics in return for one or two sacrifices and allowed popular idioms themselves to be revitalized. The Latin of the humanists contained the evolution—which was also the dissolution—of the languages that developed from Vulgar Latin. That is the lesson provided by the study of patois and argot. Literary and scientific languages are rehabilitated in the process.

—February 17, 1944

The Romance of Mademoiselle Aïssé

Compared to Heloïse, Louise Labé, or Marianna Alcoforado, Mademoiselle Aïssé seems rather a pale shadow.[1] Nonetheless, she has her place in the history of the passions, commanding our attention by her modesty and enduring while seeming to have been forgotten. Her charm lies in the melancholy fate of one who was neither totally happy nor truly unhappy. There is something quixotic about her destiny that contrasts with her tranquility of spirit and her love of plain and simple joys. All she wants to be is natural, and she is interesting. She desires a love that is innocent, and she condemns herself to being guilty. Entirely free of literary pretentions, she survives enduringly in a literary half-light. It is as if her life is revealed by her discretion and immortalized by her reserve. Posterity is drawn to her for the way she eludes it.

Her origins play a major role in the poetry of her romance. Was she a princess? Did she spend her early years in a palace? The fact that she had survived the destruction of a Circassian town and as a four-year-old girl had found herself being sold in a slave market, where she was bought by the French ambassador, M. de Ferriol, was enough to appeal to the imagination and captivate a society whose refinements she acquired without being corrupted by them. The fate from which she was rescued and that gives her story such piquancy also casts an uneasy shadow over it. The little Circassian girl is the delight of high society, which is aware of her origins, but her status as an outsider proves an obstacle to the happiness she dreams of, even perhaps a source of the most dreadful misfortune. It is all too clear for what pleasures her master gave her an education after saving her from degradation and made her resemble a girl from the respectable nobility. Fate has decreed, he wrote to her one day, that you should be my daughter and my mistress, since I am unable to distinguish between love and friendship, or between ardent passion and paternal love. Was fate heeded? Were the cunning and the virtuousness of a very young girl enough to defend her against it? One could deliberate at length, as Sainte-Beuve did, about this deplorable ransom.[2] What she is left with at least is the inconvenience of an ambiguous situation, and the feeling that she is not quite what she appears to be.

At twenty-seven, she fell in love with the chevalier d'Aydie and loved only him. For his part, the chevalier loved her in the most delicate and tender fashion, and even when she was dead, he remained faithful to her by becoming passionately attached to the daughter she gave him, whom he recognized, raised, and provided with a good match. In this passion there are none of the bursts of anger that make discord the proof of concord; there is something entirely natural about the harmony between this couple, which stems from a shared outlook, the same sense of delicacy and a sensibility that time never jades. Right to the end, Aïssé cannot find words to celebrate the passion he lavishes on her. "In matters of love I am the happiest person in the world," she writes. And later: "He speaks to me in the most tender, passionate and enthusiastic courtly language." And a few days before her death she receives this assurance from him: "I think that nothing will detract from my happiness for as long as you allow me to see myself and to flatter myself, just as you see me, as the gentleman who is most attached to you." This love has something perfect about it, it is admirable, it unites two beings who have everything in common. And yet it is shrouded in a vague sadness that gently prevents it from being happy. Because we know about this love only from the correspondence between Aïssé and one of her friends, Madame Calandrini, a very virtuous Swiss lady who was very rational and ill disposed toward passion, it is not easy to follow its twists and turns or to get to the heart of a melancholy that remains undeclared. Why did the young woman not marry the chevalier? He had offered to marry her, and marriage was her profoundest wish, both for her daughter's sake and for her own salvation, and also in order to be true to a love that needed to be open and suffered from being guilty. Despite her wishes, she rejected the offer he made; she persistently refused what she constantly desired. She wished to do nothing that might harm him and cause him to regret his actions mater. "Whatever happiness it might give me to marry him, I must love the chevalier for himself. . . . I have too much respect for his reputation, but I also have too much pride to allow him to do commit such a folly. . . . He would certainly regret having yielded to his wild passion, and I could not survive the pain of being the cause of his misfortune, and being no longer loved by him."

This decision, which reflects the fine sentimental traditions of the seventeenth century (and of the Regency period), caused her a secret chagrin, as well as regrets and qualms. By refusing marriage out of a belief in honor, she also refused virtue, and this made her think that in the name of virtue she must now sacrifice love. That is the advice of her austere correspondent, who has influence over her and who condemns the irregular nature of her liaison. Poor Aïssé now lives in a state of agitation and uncertainty. She is just as in love with the chevalier as she always was, and for his part he is responsive to all her demands. But this sentiment appears to her to lead nowhere. She is no longer capable of calmly accepting his love, and she lacks the courage to reject him. "How can I brutally put an end to such violent passion, to this most tender and justified of friendships?

In addition, there is the gratitude I feel: it is terrible! Death could not be worse." At the same time her friend is reproving her, taking her to task, urging her to make an effort. She struggles, then falls ill. During her last months, it is not clear whether she is seriously weakened because she has deprived herself of love or whether being close to death has already released her from love. Her struggle itself remains discreet, almost gentle. The tragedy is silent; the violent impulses are invisible. In her last letter, having made the decision to end the relationship, she says to the man she loves: "No one has ever seen such violent passion, more delicacy, more sentiment, more nobility and generosity." This can be applied exactly to her own fate, which, be it joy or misfortune, grants her nothing that does not stem from the purest sort of modesty and self-effacement.

Aïssé's letters have been published more than once. The edition that Marcel Arland has just given us in the delightful "À la promenade" series will gain her a new following.[3] She never disappoints, and readers find pleasure in these simple letters, out of friendship for their heroine above all, but also because she writes most agreeably and often portrays the world she moves in with considerable acumen. There is much that is natural in these letters, as in all those that were written in the eighteenth century, but there is also perhaps a little more sensibility, a sincerer and more ingenuous tendency, and a greater innocence of spirit. She is clear-sighted about the society that is hers. She knows what goes on in it. Madame de Parabère and Madame Du Deffand are her friends. But be it her innocent gaze or the delicacy of her sentiments, she takes part in these exchanges with a certain reserve and seems to be saving herself for the true passion she has chosen. In other words, at all times what we read is the chronicle of a loving heart who is guided by tenderness and who, amid the din of a scandalous and cynical century, seeks diffidently to reconcile passion, virtue, and silence.

—February 24, 1944

The Joy of Storytelling

Marce Aymé's books have the good fortune to make even the subtlest of critical explanations appear crude. What they are makes a mockery of everything that can be said about them. When read, they charm their reader; subsequent analysis remains under the spell of this grace, and even if it looks at the back of the tapestry and points out the skill of the workmanship and the originality of the weave, it is to no avail.

Yet *The Fable and the Flesh* is a novel that can also be admired for its artful insouciance.[1] It is about the Vouivre, a girl out of fable who belongs to the mythology of Franche-Comté. She is both a wood nymph and a water nymph, and she bathes in the rivers and wanders the hills and valleys of the Jura. In her hair she wears a brilliant diadem, which contains a ruby that is the finest precious stone you could ever see. She removes it only when she bathes, leaving it on the riverbank with her robe. Whoever tries to take it is immediately set upon by vipers, who deprive the thief of all hope of ever enjoying the fruits of his pilfering. The Vouivre is the snake-girl. In Marcel Aymé's book she appears in the flesh to the villagers of Vaux-le Devers, and for a few months she disturbs the peace of village life with her marvels. In reality, people's imaginations are aroused not so much by the miraculous fact that she exists as by the extraordinary wealth of which she is sometimes the source. A few hotheads dream of stealing her ruby. The vicar himself sees this apparition as merely a pretext for taking revenge on the anticlerical town hall and for demanding a solemn procession. Only the freethinking mayor finds his convictions powerfully shaken. In short, the presence of the Vouivre causes hardly a ripple. Each person responds to her according to his habits and his instincts. All people see in her is themselves.

A familiar feature of Marcel Aymé's writing is his way of combining a very faithful and realistic portrait of things with an original inventiveness that is purely fantastical. This inventiveness brooks no justification. It asks for none, indeed it cannot conceive of such a thing. Authors who are drawn to what is unrealistic often try to follow the example of Edgar Allan Poe and acclimatize the impossible, suggest a natural explanation for it, and allow ambiguity to surround the strange events that either disrupt or do not disrupt the ordinary course of events, depending on the reader. Marcel Aymé has no time at all for such hypocritical expedients. He calmly asserts the existence of the extraordinary, and his merit lies first and foremost in the lack of precaution with which he offers it to us. To begin to explain the inexplicable is to admit that it could be called into doubt. The author of *The Wonderful Farm* does not allow us such reservations.[2] He does not try to lull our minds with heavy-handed preliminaries, he just tells us what is what; we are won over by the solidity of his self-assurance. We therefore have to believe in the Vouivre, like the country folk of Vaux-le-Devers, and not be astonished by her. Above all, we must not provide her with alibis. Another author would have immediately looked for ways of disguising her: The Vouivre would have been a witch with snakes as her familiars, would have been surrounded by the trappings of rustic devil worship, and as the child of popular credulity would have sought to appeal to ours. But a writer with a sense of what is natural is careful not to resort to such calculated ploys, so as not to awaken our skepticism by returning us to an order of things where everything must be justified.

Marcel Aymé's country folk appear very simple and devoid of mystery. They obey their instincts; they are hardworking, avaricious, and taciturn; tradition finds them exactly where it left them. And yet beneath their clearly drawn outlines there is something subtle and delicate going on that gives their appearance a sort of depth. It is clear that, in *The Vouivre*, the truly mysterious people are the country folk, Arsène Muselier for example, who is hard, self-centered, feels no compunction about having an inconvenient rival killed, but in whom childhood memories can elicit a sensibility that is pure and restrained. This Arsène has an affair with the Vouivre. Instead of eying up her ruby, he has been watching the girl and been aroused—and also somewhat abashed—by the sight of her well-proportioned body. In fact, his relations with her are in no way extraordinary; if at times he finds what this somewhat abnormal being confides to him disturbing, he is more often inconvenienced by the attention she lavishes on him, and far from yielding to the giddy flights of an exclusive passion, his interest in her lasts only as long as a brief fling. If anyone could find reasons to be astonished about the affair, it would be the mischievous girl who, though she has known the people of the Jura for eons, often finds their way of being incomprehensible, and as an immortal, wonders in vain what meaning they can give to their labors, their down-to-earth lives, and their deaths. But she does not let herself be distracted by futile enigmas. She is like the country folk in that she no more asks superfluous questions than they do; and like them, when things happen she is always simultaneously there and not there in relation to them.

Few writers in our literature produce more delightful humor than Marcel Aymé. He sometimes brings to mind the wit of Alphonse Daudet, but he is simpler, more discreet, less in tune with literary fashion. An infinite capacity for subtle sympathy reveals to him the candid face that humans always retain, and that is always visible to those who love them. Even the most impure urges retain an element of delectable innocence, and they merge in his mirror with the gentlest of images. His robust language is courtesy itself. Crude indecency has the luster of delicate refinement. He likes what he depicts, and however extravagant or harsh, his portraits always have the authenticity and gentleness that come from his sympathy. His style is without affectation and full of calm equanimity. He is without pretense, gains our attention without subterfuge, and even refuses to resort to imagery. He is loyal and restrained. His civility lies in his modesty, which makes him conceal the enchanter the better to reveal the enchantment.

One of the charming things about these tales is that it is impossible to fill them with symbols. They are simply what they appear. Any meaning we attribute to them is a debasement, when compared to the unapologetic pleasures that they give us. Naturally however, some readers will be unable to resist the temptation to interpret them. They will see in the Vouivre a nostalgia for childhood that will eventually unsettle a countryman as levelheaded as Arsène Muselier. He quarrels with his brother, cuts himself off from his family, abandons all hope for the good marriage he had planned, and even loses the will to work. When he finally dies after being bitten by the snakes, it is not through coveting the precious stone—which would be a normal, healthy passion—but because he came to the assistance of a shepherdess who retains in his eyes the allure of childhood sentiment. Summed up in this way, the story appears rather heavy-handed. In the novel, it is lightness itself. It comes and it goes, taking you with it as it pleases. It is indistinguishable from those real and unreal, mysterious and incontrovertible people, the country folk of the Jura and the fabulous Vouivre.

—March 2, 1944

Outlawed Idols

Although Paul Valéry's reputation is immense and appreciated by all the best writers, it has perhaps never earned the crowning accolade that critical commentators might have been expected to grant it. Of course, he has been written about endlessly, and a number of major volumes are even quite well done. But the reader of these innumerable publications has the impression that they are always less clear and less explicit than their subject, and in a word generally unnecessary. The reason for this is clear. At its inception, the work already had its commentator, one that rendered all other reflection redundant and made the sharpest attention and the most lucid scrutiny seem feeble and vague. Paul Valéry's work provides its own commentary. It exists solely to allow the mind that created it to reflect on it and to reflect itself through it. It provides that mind with the means to verify itself. All those who come after that essential effort of approximation and contestation appear as no more than desultory historians.

It is understandable therefore that in *The Presence of Paul Valéry*, André Berne-Joffroy's thoughts should be preceded by "Words about Me," written by Valéry himself.[1] There are notes about everything in these "words," but they mainly concern the writer's intellectual preferences and his method. There are also—and this is less common in a man who held anecdote in such disdain—a number of revelations concerning his moods. To be fair, it should be added that in this partial portrait, the author only shows his face personally in order to minimize biographical circumstance and link his personal particulars to his work routine. For example, he lays great stress on his bad memory; incapable of retaining a text, forgetful of names, faces, and events, it is reliable only when it comes to ideas, or more precisely, to certain ways of handling ideas. It avoids pure facts, and it is drawn to the movement of the mind and to certain problems. From the past it rejects what belongs to the past and retains what has value as a possibility, what is a resource placed at the disposal of the future. Hence he can write: "I do not care for memories. . . . Events bore me. . . . For me, the past is more devoid of its chronological, narratable development than it is for most people, I believe." And this observation partly explains the sort of disdain he feels for history, or at least for the sort of pretentions that this type of activity allows.

It is reasonably obvious that a writer who is so powerfully attached to the power of the intellect will have no liking for his own feelings. "How," as he puts it very finely, "can one avoid concealing oneself in order to feel?" This aversion to confession and the excesses of sensibility ("How reluctant I am to write down my 'feelings,' to note what so many people complacently put down on paper!") is not just the expression of a sensibility that finds itself abhorrent, but it corresponds above all to a concern for rigor. Feelings are vague, impure things that compromise language and discourage precision. They are "things you carry with you" for which there are no suitable words. Words can achieve some dignity only if they are an exercise of the mind, a method of calculation, or an instrument for action;

otherwise restlessly, ad infinitum, and with loathsome laxity, they churn up hidden phantoms that correspond to nothing. Whence that other aversion for big words (truth, god, justice) that try to appear more than they mean, the distaste for "opinions," the horror of "politics," the diffidence toward religions and the severe condemnation of all apologetics. "Keep proselytizing to a minimum, that is my position. I despise anyone who tries to convince me. . . . It is an offense against humanity to want all men to think the same thing."

To complete this picture of his moods, Paul Valéry finally admits certain things that must be presented as they stand: "I cannot abide serious-minded people. I cannot abide even the thought of kidneys, tripe, intestines in general; I only like meat if it is disguised. . . . I eat too quickly, I speak too quickly, I think too quickly. . . . I do not notice what there is around me, I have no need of any setting, and it is in a hotel room that is as impersonal as possible that I am most glad to work." It is also well known that the author of *Charms* rose almost every day at 4:00 in the morning, and in the purest, deepest hour between his lamp and the sun he was in the habit of writing things that invented themselves spontaneously. This labor, taking place outside the bounds of ordinary circumstance, led him to reject the ordinary view of things. "To think differently from everyone else comes almost naturally to someone who, while most people are asleep, feels acutely awake." But these needs, these peculiarities from which one may idly—and always abstractly—derive infinite consequences, and that serve to reveal the real presence of the writer, have in fact very little value when it comes to his true presence, which is entirely intellectual in nature and is summed up in this statement: I am a mind, a man of the mind.

It is this presence that André Berne-Joffroy has sought to express in the orderly, modest, if sometimes overly simple analyses that he devotes to it. There are two remarks of his that are worth noting. First of all, it seems clear to him that what lies at the center of Paul Valéry's venture, the essential persona that lives in him, is neither the writer nor the poet but the person he calls Valéry-Teste, or using a less congenial term, the thinker. It seems to him too that whatever the degree of influence that Mallarmé may have had on the author of the *Young Fate*, the relations between the two writers remain unclear, and that his effective predecessors are Descartes and Edgar Allan Poe. All that is clear, and probably close to the truth. But the link to Descartes creates more problems than it solves. A more specific study of the figure of Valéry-Teste would examine why, however prudent his analysis and rigorous his language, the assertion of the primacy of the intellect that is crucial in his eyes remains ambiguous, complacent, and corrupted by the vagueness of the spoken word. Where does this impression of ambiguity originate? Paul Valéry knows perfectly well that the values he is attached to are based on a set of assumptions: By outlawing the idols of sensibility, he has perhaps arbitrarily, but in full accord with himself, created another idol, that he calls the Idol of intellect, and as this name indicates, he attributes to it no transcendent reality, no substantial truth. He also explained many times that there is nothing mysterious about what he means by the mind: It is a specific power of transformation that may be studied independently of its results, or, more precisely, whose value is not linked to the contingency of the matter it transforms, and whose sole precision lies in the fact that it is a means of action, a calculation, an exercise. For Paul Valéry, the mind is simply a set of means, and those means always appear more interesting to him than all of the ends that they allow him to achieve, or else the ends are primarily of interest to him only with reference to the means deployed in order to reach them. However, the ambiguity remains. The mind alternately identifies with consciousness in general (it is in that sense that he writes, "Everything that comes to mind is what constitutes mind itself"); or else it merges with its clear point of concentration, the place where consciousness reflects on itself, and from where he believes that all the products of art and science flow; or else it becomes a power that is reconstituted from its most rigorous products, the mathematical and mechanical sciences. That is no doubt where the great ambiguity in Valéry's analyses lies. Like Descartes, he felt the attraction of the rigorous ideal represented by certain of the sciences. And like him, he hovered between a notion of consciousness reduced to its "appearances," and a notion of the mind that "is" what it is capable of, for which the ideal of precision and exactitude, in short, the truth must necessarily lie on the side of some of its manifestations at the expense of certain others.

To a certain extent, the movement of Paul Valéry's thought has affinities with that of phenomenology. It too presupposes the primacy of consciousness, but rather than spontaneous consciousness, it is consciousness that seeks to overcome itself in reflection, rediscover itself in its flight, capture itself in a gaze whose specific value he asserts. But at the same time, he does not confine himself to what lies within the mind. He implicitly admits that a certain scientific perspective on the mind—that is to say, when it is seen from without—is equally valid. He borrows his ideal of truth from a mode of being that is perhaps foreign to that of consciousness, and which in any case he seeks to impose on it uncritically and without scrutiny. This contradiction, the constant movement between one point of view and another (by the term "mind" he understands both the mind seen from within and the mind seen from without), compromises the most powerful analyses and those definitions that are least prone to the aberrations of language. It explains in part how Paul Valéry's influence has remained primarily literary, despite the extraordinary celebrity of M. Teste.

—March 9, 1944

The Art of André Dhôtel

Some novels could not be more secretive. They are simple and modest. They stay close to reality and tell of lives that are perfectly ordinary. The source of the intense pleasure that comes from reading them lies neither in the way their story is put together, nor in the way it is told. How is it that we become so seriously attached to them, as though they were profound, and ingenuously take an interest in them, as though they possessed the skill of the perfectly told story? Perhaps they charm us by being calculating in all innocence, and simple thanks to an art that is both sure of itself and self-aware.

André Dhôtel is an exceptional writer and worthy of serious note. He probably has no interest in being read by large numbers of people, provided he is appreciated by the few that he respects. His way of writing displays a reserve that does not adapt easily to being applauded too intensely, but his novels definitely have more qualities than many celebrated works, and make us remember them and accept them more readily than those works do. A few months ago we discussed his *Pathetic*

Village, a book that was still unsure of itself and dissatisfied with its own plot, but that possessed a purity of tone and an insouciant delicacy that made it precious.[1] His new novel, which he has entitled *Nowhere*, is a much more accomplished work.[2] We are carried away when we read it. We are eager for the diversions it offers. We believe in the events that it narrates. If these merits are perhaps superficial ones, they enhance the novel's authenticity and make it pleasurable without distorting it.

Dhôtel's books contain a secret. That secret does not consist of a message he wishes to convey, and that he conceals beneath the pleasures that fiction offers. Rather, it concerns his art and the nature of his characters. While in no way obscure, these characters are quite impenetrable. But the resistance they offer does not as such allow us to be entirely certain about it. On the contrary, there are many reasons for thinking that this young innkeeper, these petty bourgeois folk, this violent smuggler and these bad-mannered youngsters have nothing mysterious about them that escapes our eye. The author does not engage us in a battle of wits. Methodically, clearly, and honestly, he tells us everything there is to tell and everything that he knows about the people he describes. What is more, his heroes make no claim to be extraordinary, and their adventures do not take them away from the sort of experiences in which we are able to accompany them. Rather, they adopt a mechanical air, as though they were always obeying perfectly simple instincts, as though the motive of their actions and even of their thoughts could never entirely escape thorough analysis. Yet it is here that their mysterious side appears. They are inflexible, blunt, and elusive. They can be taken apart and explored like perfect little machines, but their natural clarity opens onto something indefinably unknown and unpredictable. At the same time, the hidden anarchy in such automatic behavior does not conflict with their perfectly precise character, and it is not added on artificially to their perfect coherence. If they fail to do what it would be plausible to expect them to do, this occurs discreetly.

They resemble lucid, determined beings whom we suspect (but only suspect) of acting haphazardly and unthinkingly.

André Dhôtel's universe is one where chance does indeed exist as a benevolent and baleful force, one that is difficult to adapt to and that people try to win over through a curious combination of inertia, tenacity, effort, and indolence. First of all, they scarcely say anything about what matters to them most. This silence is no doubt part of their discreet way of being, and it comes from the fact that their dream eludes the clear vision they have of themselves; they are content to say as one of them does in the vaguest possible manner, which is as vague as what they experience: it would be nice to be in a thrilling situation. But their indecision and the silence that ultimately conceals what they want also help to work out a solution to the thorny problems that exercise them. They wander through a precisely defined world, never quite knowing what they are in search of, focusing on minor details that are of no interest (but that are in reality rich in significance for an understanding of their secret), and lost in serious thoughts that lead to nothing. When in the course of these activities that are both justified and futile, a chance encounter suddenly reveals to them what they desire—a girl, a freer life, the chance of an affair—they often make a determined effort to obtain it, but more often than not too this effort causes them to fail. And in that case, they do not persist, but instead go back to their neatly ordered lives; they start to wait again, tranquilly and hopefully, for the chance that will bring them closer to the phantom they have glimpsed. They are neither strong-willed not irresolute; they have simply understood that the best way of grappling with events lies in courteously fading into the background, deferring any decision and placing themselves modestly in the hands of the indeterminate, absent force we call fortune. Naturally, there is nothing optimistic about this outlook: Chance is not always a faithful servant, and the smuggler who hides in the sand while patiently waiting for the police to leave, or for some stroke of luck to turn up, is finally crushed by a container dropped by a crane swinging haphazardly above his head. In itself, this outcome is not particularly important. What matters is perhaps not success, but a sort of deference toward fate, a precise and painstaking indolence that gives its due to the ineffable, and also a conscious surrender, without resignation or discouragement, to universal caprice.

One of the charms of these books lies in what is ordinary and unexpected about their detail, and in themes that, however modest, reflect the profound interest that their author takes in them. In both *The Pathetic Village* and *Nowhere* we see two beings who, while perfectly destined for each other, rebuff, flee, and then go looking for each other in vain despite the complicity of the world. It is only after a long journey through a variety of feelings, and thanks to the complex, risky interplay of circumstances, that they find each other and become sure of each other. During their quest, they are generally attracted to milieus that social barriers exclude them from, and by strange callings for which they are not prepared. In marrying his cousin, Jacques Brostier could become a wealthy landowner, but he prefers to hang around with small-time riff-raff or dabble in smuggling, and he ends up with a market stall selling optical instruments. Small trades play a big role in this world. Perhaps the ingenuous picture we are given of them conveys a somewhat artificial impression. What used to be called magical realism has made us very wary of those ersatz emotions that writers who were in search of renewal once looked for in life seen as a popular spectacle. Wandering journeymen proved a dubious fashion that faded even more quickly than the themes of proletarian and populist literature. André Dhôtel is saved from such errors by the development of his characters and the reality of the landscapes in which he brings them to life. Almost all his book is set in Béthune. He has provided an unaffected and memorable portrait of this mediocre town, the empty lots of its suburbs and the neighboring countryside, crisscrossed by streets, pavements, and urban architecture. It is evident that the writer has sought to describe precisely only what he has seen, and this minute precision has allowed him to connect the strange world he imagines with the world he knows, as if each of them must henceforth appear inseparable to our eyes.

—March 16, 1944

Balzac's Way of Working

The life of Balzac in two volumes that André Billy has just published takes as its epigraphs this remark by Théophile Gautier: "No one can ever hope to write a complete biography of Balzac," and this proud claim by the author of *Old Goriot*: "I am inexplicable to everyone, no one possesses the secret of my life and I will reveal it to no one."[1] Billy's book displays all of the qualities we can expect from a writer who loves, knows, and sometimes reminds us of Balzac by the way he writes his novels. It also displays all the modesty of such a writer. The biographer's sole wish is to tell of a life that, at almost every moment, finds expression simultaneously in a whole variety of events, acquires complexity the more it produces, is blighted by alarming financial ventures, and yet appears simple, so violently and urgently impulsive that we ultimately see in it an incomparable degree of precision and clarity in the midst of all its extraordinary machinations. Billy has said almost everything, and rather than become bogged down in a morass of episodes, his story successfully follows the movement that is driving it and whose mysterious constraint it perfectly conveys. No doubt he leaves aside the problems posed by most of Balzac's activities. Not that these are strange or defy explanation; rather, they are those of a man who, in certain respects and however much he may be a creator, yields to his simple capacity for living, appearing always to be beyond literature or else beneath its threshold, yet who in other respects seems entirely under the sway of his work and is indistinguishable from it, having established an enigmatic relation between the incidents of his daily life and the forms found in his works.

It is well known that an entire area of Balzac's life coincides with his work. But though we know the habits, the schedule, and the stimulants associated with this work, we remain ignorant of much of what we would particularly like to know about: the peculiar workings of his intellect, the procedures he imagined for improving them through constant modifications, and the mysterious interplay between his projects and his literary action. One of the best-known aspects is the abundance of his corrections. Balzac preserved almost nothing of what he wrote at a first sitting. Not only did he cross things out, write above the line and change things perpetually, he sometimes replaced one version entirely with another, rewrote the same work ten or fifteen times, and once it appeared to be finished, changed the chapters around, modified their order unpredictably and obtained a rigorous composition through an almost random process of encounters and coincidences. This was an indescribable labor, writes Billy, and one that could be compared to nothing except a card game in which the cards were shuffled and reshuffled seemingly at random, until the order of the parts acquired a meaning. There is a further highly significant detail: Many of these arrangements were carried out at proof stage, while the text was going to print. As soon as the writer was able to read himself in type (*en lettres moulées*) he found a new basis for his efforts. The material was more solid, a greater effort was required in order to resist it, and this difficulty prompted Balzac to take a different view of his work, freeing it from the looseness and indecision of its initial form, like a sculptor who abandons clay for stone. This way of working certainly reflects a profound necessity. It does not only point to a high degree of perfectionism, or a dislike of easy tasks; it must also be linked to the secret of his "inspiration." Balzac does not produce a book in a dream state, he invents things only if he is writing. Meditating to no effect means nothing to him. Were he to be deprived of ink, paper, and momentarily of words, his mind would go to sleep, and in its darkness there would not even be the outline of a Balzacian world. *The Unknown Masterpiece* provides an illustration of the awareness he has of the creative power of work, and of the excesses that would extinguish that power if it were not governed by material constraints. In this well-known story a famous painter who is rich, free of cares, and who, to make things more dangerous, has ideas, exhausts himself by retouching his work and in the process, destroying it. "This sublime painter," says Porbus to the young Poussin as they contemplate the disaster of a masterpiece destroyed by its own perfection, "had the misfortune to be born rich, and this allowed his mind to wander. Do not imitate him! Work! Painters should philosophize only when they have a brush in their hand."

These words of advice explain how Balzac went about his work. Art has little to do with the mind. It constantly asks to be put to the test through action. It begins only when it is happening, and everything that takes the form of abstract preparation, thinking about an idea, or feasting on ideals encourages the artist to count for nothing. You must philosophize with a brush in your hand, and for a prose writer, thinking begins only once words have been written down, sentences linked to other sentences, and once he has yielded to the heavy demand of writing that makes thought real by altering its function. Balzac needs a material presence, and, as Alain so rightly says, those accumulations into which his prose plunges in order to gradually take shape. The printed proofs that he uses to work are "a sort of plastic outline imprinted in matter."

Through the intervention of something real he wards off the danger of fanciful thinking, puts an end to the pursuit of words that do not exist, and rejects the lure of a beauty that would be nothing but absence.

It would appear that Balzac also discovered one of the central ideas of his work in this requirement imposed by his mind. We know that he encounters it while he is writing *The Magic Skin*: It is then that he sees the idea that will give its significance to his entire work, and with the aid of which he will explore social reality from now on, and this idea is the destructive power of thought. Balzac feels a sort of terror at the power of a thought that does not take on flesh, that dominates the passions and becomes an obsession, so turning the joyful mobility of human life into a destiny. The novelist's creativity, like social existence, is endangered by the power that gives rise to it; its main enemy is what provides it with its justification; it is infinitely suspicious of the meaning it gives itself. And that is certainly true of Balzac's own art, for obsession is not just the mark of his heroes but also the mark of his creativity. It risks confining it within a structure that is too logical, and it loses its abstract character only through the excess to which it leads and which, illuminated by an extremely powerful imagination, makes it ceases to be an idea and become a passion. This recalls the criticism he directed at Stendhal: "It would be too dangerous to allow authors to believe they are profound thinkers." It is against that danger that he guards himself instinctively; he has identified it in all of its forms and kept an eye on all of its angles, because he has experienced it as an obsession. (It is this danger once again that he describes in *Gambara*, in which a musician loses his talent through composing according to theoretical ideas, rather than out of a proper devotion to sounds.)

It should be noted that Balzac attributes the downfall of the painter in the *Unknown Masterpiece* to the fortune that left him with too much leisure. It is all too clear that what the writer was doing there was vaunting his own money problems. Billy sees his debts as one of the principal spurs to his genius.

They forced him to work, but more than that, he was intoxicated and infatuated by them, held in a trancelike state in which he became fully himself: "He needed debts in order to work the way others need alcohol or opium." It is as if his genius conjured up inextricable obstacles for itself in order to provide itself with some balance. Without looming payment dates, would he ever have abandoned his anguished revisions? According to Georges Guénot, who observed him at work at the Croissant printers, "his idleness, or perhaps better his fears, his indecisiveness, his anxieties when it came to picking up his pen were so great that, whether with his diary or his books, he would make himself go on working up to very last minute." And this is one of the most prodigiously productive of writers that literature has ever produced, and seemingly one of the fastest! But he was simultaneously infinitely slow and infinitely swift. Haste and excessive work were the resources he needed to go on working. His energy increased the more he expended it. In short, the material act of creation was all that saved him from what he saw as the misfortune of thinking.

—March 23, 1944

The Gothic Novel

The publisher José Corti has brought out a new edition of Horace Walpole's *The Castle of Otranto*, with a brief preface by Paul Éluard.[1] It is a novel whose success in England gave rise to the gothic novel (*roman noir*). Much has been written about the causes, the tendencies, and the mysterious effects of this literary mode, which has recently begun to flourish again. The gothic novel is not the same thing as fantastic literature. If it sets great store by the marvelous, its primary goal is to act on the emotions using the stock in trade of terror. It seeks to stir up the imagination. It sweeps it up in a frenetic movement that allows it no rest. It incites it to believe everything except for happy outcomes and cozy compromises, using means whose conventional nature further increases their power. It is a methodical art that is aware of how crude it is, and it often uses this to create subtle effects.

For about fifty years, beginning in 1764 when *The Castle of Otranto* appeared, literary society in England, France, and Germany was infatuated with the plots found in novels of terror. This craze has even been considered a phenomenon whose literary dimension is not what is most noteworthy about it. Before the Revolution as well as after it, minds played at tragedy, and abnormal experiences that sometimes ended in funereal extravagance reflected this need for horror that literature stimulated without satisfying it. It is worth noting that this eruption of the supernatural occurs when the age of rationalism is at its zenith. The Horace Walpole who gives free rein to phantoms is a friend of the Encyclopedists, and Hume is a close acquaintance. It is true that the eighteenth century was also the era of the Count de Saint-Germain, of Mesmer, Cazotte, the unknown philosopher, and many others. The esoteric tradition of the Illuminati would have provided the frenetic novel with a guarantee for its mysteries, were its strangeness more often than not devoid of content and incompatible with any form of intellectual transposition.

The great works associated with the gothic novel may well have few readers nowadays, because most of them are out of print, but they have acquired a significant place in literary history. Names like Clara Reeve, Ann Radcliffe, *The Mysteries of Udolpho*, and *A Sicilian Romance* are familiar to us, as are others such as Lewis, whose three-volume novel *The Monk* provides a near-comprehensive view of fantastic literature as a genre, and Maturin, whose *Melmoth or the Traveller* influenced Baudelaire. These authors can be considered close enough to each other to be indistinguishable, except in terms of imagination and talent. However, Maurice Heine has suggested a classification that at least has the advantage of showing up every shade of black, as well as the different pathways taken by horror.[2] The oldest and basically purest tradition is that of gothic horror, and its model is *The Castle of Otranto*. It is linked to the medieval revival, and the Romanticism that will rehabilitate medieval themes is directly influenced by it. What is remarkable about this tradition is the extraordinary use it makes of the basic setting. In certain respects it is normal for authors to situate these stories with their use and abuse of phantoms in a period when such phenomena are in principle more widespread. It is thus a simple concern for realism that explains this choice in the first instance. Castles, chapels, and suits of armor are merely materials whose use is required because of the recourse to a legendary version of the Middle Ages. Soon, however, under the influence of objective imagination, these elements reveal a real power of enchantment. They cast a spell; they exert a charm. They appear laden with poetic value. They function as a signal and trigger the forces that these novels seek to unleash. These underground passages, these towers, these eternally forbidden rooms truly are haunted by the poetry of fright. It is not the tragedies for which they provide the theater that make them uninhabitable; it is the indefinable mystery that gives the dramas their baleful nature. As Paul Éluard writes, the true heroes are the objects. In *The Castle of Otranto* the gigantic helmet, a hundred times larger than a normal one, covered in a mass of black feathers and beneath which the prince's young son is mysteriously buried, is more than just a disturbing image: It is an empty, absurd presence, an approximate reality that brings discredit to the most ordinary things from the everyday world and suggests that in the cold substance of the objects we use there lies an affinity with what is strange from which we could all well die.

From this region where terror arises from things that have escaped the bounds of use, from this undated era that coincides only by chance with history, fantastic writers have often made their escape by setting their fictions in the architecture and the landscapes of their era. This shift of site does have its drawbacks. The ghosts of the Restoration find it difficult to enter a boudoir. Deprived of their ruins they vanish, and the novelists lack the talent for accommodating monsters by making them more important and more true-to-life than the places where they appear. On the contrary, what Maurice Heine calls dark realism, which excludes the intervention of supernatural beings and derives all of its resources from madness or unknown natural forces (such as magnetism), finds a place more easily in the modern periods. But now the drama requires the assistance of psychology and analysis; it is authentic only if it avoids what is conventional. We are a long way from the traditional genre that seeks its truth in artifice and has no wish to paint what is unbelievable in precise colors. And in the ultimate metamorphosis of an art that declines as it grows subtler, irony and caricature take over the impossible situations of the gothic novel. They claim not to be fooled by them, and they playfully exaggerate them. But humor has a talent for playing with terror without dispelling it: Where does playfulness begin, and where does it end? Burlesque gothic tries to revive the old plots and to perturb the imagination one last time by exposing it to ambiguity.

Dominique Corticchiato, who has very skillfully interpreted every nuance of the text, takes a stern view of the novel he has translated. It is true that *The Castle of Otranto* often appears to be a cold and superficial work. Did Horace Walpole really write it in an hour of unconscious inspiration, as he claimed? There is scarcely any sign of this, and today what we perceive is the mark of a calculating and methodical mind, combining together devices it does not believe in, rather than the deranged actions of an imagination in thrall to its errors. However, its well-organized character seems indisputably linked to the genre itself. The gothic novel resembles tragedy, of which it is a continuation, and the detective novel, which it anticipates through the rigor of its methods and its adhesion to its own precepts. Chance does not guide the reader toward the fear he wishes to enjoy. Fear is presented, then inflicted on him methodically. He must only tremble according to the rules. Historically, *The Castle of Otranto* remains admirable because of the perfect way in which it anticipates all the forms of the genre it invents. Almost all of the themes and all of the methods that will later be developed are already in use in this little book. Not just the décor, the objects, and the supernatural mythology but also the fate that punishes the innocent along with the guilty, the futility of love, death as the supreme misunderstanding, defiant pride that is unimpressed by wonders, and all those episodes of human misery in which an indefatigable public will seek its pleasure, all find a place in this fiction, and for half a century they will be handed on from book to book almost unaltered. Horace Walpole is much more than a precursor. He genuinely appears to be the author of the thousands of books that stem from him. This slimmest of volumes makes him the most prolific of writers.

—March 30, 1944

The Secrets of the Dream

Although systematic studies of dreams have proliferated over the last fifty years—Freud's first major work dates from 1900—to most people's minds, our oneiric activity appears more like an enigma than a problem on the way to being solved. Conflicting solutions remain equally possible. Paul Valéry had no hesitation about casting doubt on the existence of dreams; others adhere to the long-established view of Hervy de Saint-Denys, for whom there is no sleep without dreams; some agree with Maury that dreams constitute a short burst of mental activity occurring equally when we are awake and when we are asleep. Scores of theories devoted to the simple question of the space occupied by our dreams continue to divide opinion among those who pursue research on the subject. And yet it is clear that no phenomenon has interested mankind more constantly or preoccupied its spirit of observation more persistently. Hegel recalls that after he had destroyed the gates of Pavia with his canon and destroyed the last pockets of rebellion, Napoleon's sole concern during a visit to the university was to put to a class that was studying ideology the thorny question of the difference between waking and sleeping. As André Breton has pointed out, it is remarkable to see a conqueror who has just changed the course of events quizzing a handful of people who have no real means of providing an answer on the subject of the activities of his nocturnal imagination, as though, at this fateful hour, he needed others to decide for him what was more important: monumental historical episodes or the "immaterial fog" of his nights.[1]

Luc Durtain in his turn has asked himself all these questions in a brilliant, serious book entitled *The Secrets of the Dream*.[2] This essay develops methodically, like a scientific work, and provides a survey of the principal studies that have been devoted in abundance to the subject, either to make use of them or to contradict them. As we know, the author divides his time between medical practice and a life of letters, and his book has the twin virtues of artistic curiosity and a degree of rigor in the way that dreams are noted down and methodically interpreted. Over a period of twenty years, Luc Durtain has scrutinized his dreams, copying them down on wakening and searching through the incidents of his recent or distant past for ways of understanding them. He has examined their laws and developed a theory designed to explain their deepest nature. What is most interesting about this effort is perhaps the intention that inspired it. The writer's concern has been to portray himself through his dreams. What he offers is the experience of a lifetime, as he puts it, a nocturnal biography that is almost complete, and he thinks that from this unadorned account, this work of darkness that seems to take shape unbeknownst to the day, there will perhaps emerge an image of himself that will be more honest, and in any case more substantial, than anything even the most faithful Memoirs could convey. The history of a life seen through its dreams is a task that no one so far has ever completed. "If a man," wrote Hebbel, "could resolve to note down all of his dreams over his entire lifetime, indiscriminately and unrestrictedly, he would present humanity with a great gift."[3] It is no doubt regrettable that, having envisaged such a large-scale experiment, Luc Durtain should have limited it to a much too modest selection that he divides up and summarizes analytically. What remains is strictly speaking no longer a history, nor a chronicle whose only visible thread is provided by the progression of his nights, the way autobiographies obey a single law of composition: the succession of each day. We are not given the extraordinary diary that would be the creation of time itself as it is lived during sleep, and in which the author himself, by placing alongside it a memento of his day-time life, would have the impression of entering a forest of transpositions, a "palace walled with mirrors"[4] whose enchantment no key could dispel. Luc Durtain has preferred to use his dreams in order to understand the nature of dream, and has sketched only the faintest outline of his darkness, so abandoning what in our view is the most original part of his project.

If one were to attempt to establish from roughly what angle *The Secrets of the Dream* should be viewed, it would have to be said that the author is basically quite close to Bergson. Like Bergson, he believes that dream is the spontaneous resurgence of authentic fragments of consciousness; more than just a function of memory, dreaming is a moment in our duration, and what it represents and brings back to life with a veracity that looks like a lie to memory when it is distorted by logic, is the precise way in which inner events produced repercussions in us. The fabric of our nocturnal life is formed from our deepest subjectivity. It thrives on pure sensation, on unattached qualities and images, on everything that has been neglected during the day by a life given over to practical requirements, and that therefore retains an evocative power. Dream material is precisely what artistic creation uses: At the heart of sensibility in a pure state lies the source of those chance discoveries and original combinations that both the artist and the dreamer, each of whom is attracted to things that are unusable, draw on in order to construct original combinations of form and idea.

A Novel by Jarry

It is perhaps inadvisable for a writer to create a literary character who becomes his own incarnation. In fact, this situation is rather rare. It is more common for an author to forge a type that will live on after him, but without expressing himself through it: once thinks of Alphonse Daudet and Tartarin, for example, or Cervantes and Don Quixote.[1] Occasionally too, a writer may become his own myth, and in this image saved from chance, revive some of the features of the heroes he has brought to life; a case in point is the aging Goethe, who feels a kinship with his Faust, yet always remains distinct from him, and in the end appears as a richer and more representative figure than he is. Then there is Rimbaud, who illustrates for all eternity the splendor of the poet who becomes a fable and a myth by refusing to be a poet. Becoming the character one has created is a more dubious fate. The merging of Henri Monnier and Joseph Prudhomme was not detrimental to the author.[2] It seems clear, though, that by persistently being Old Ubu, Jarry squandered part of his literary talent during his lifetime and led critical opinion to misjudge his true literary worth after his death.

It is strange that this dual incarnation, in the case of both Monnier and Jarry, should have led the two authors to identify not with some grand figure, but with a comical, physically repulsive being, the epitome of ugliness, stupidity, and spite in whom alongside these deformities, through some dispiriting freak of chance, most of the features of modern humanity are to be found. Why Jarry chose such an unflattering mask is plain to see. First, there is his intention to undermine everything serious, beginning with that intention itself. There is no question of keeping ridicule within certain bounds; laughter is first of all directed against oneself, and that is because such laughter is merely an echo of the void. Moreover, the grotesque double that the author flaunts as a projection he is proud of, proclaims his brazen and defiant complicity with the failings he is caricaturing. As a hero, Ubu turns every comic perspective upside down: he is the vulgarity, the cowardice, and the filth that heap derision on every higher virtue whose negative imprint they are. We think we are meant to laugh at his potbelly, suitcase, cap, umbrella, but no: That is how the superman, the potential hero, really looks. Laughter ends up as provocation.

In this mix of irreverence and ferocity we recognize a component of the modern spirit, and that is what has ensured Jarry's reputation as a precursor. Added to that, there is the ambiguity that made his work an extraliterary accident, a compromise in which literature will not necessarily receive its due. Having become Old Ubu, Alfred Jarry behaves in no way like the average writer; he lives outside of the rules and has no time for custom and practice, and legend attributes all manner of scandalous anecdotes to him that are generally false but correspond to his avowed determination to live his eccentricity and no longer just express it. In this respect he is very different from Verlaine; the main thing that these two marginals have in common is probably alcoholism, but whereas for poor Lélian, love of poetry and a life of vagrancy coexist in perfect harmony,

Jarry turns his anarchist impulses and the solitary Aunt Sally stall to which he reduced his life into more of a protest against literature, or at least a declaration of independence from it, than a poetic stimulant. The objects of his curiosity have little in common with intellectual values: He appreciates the art of heraldry, is interested in obscure scientific theories, and becomes versed in military tactics and strategy; at a time when love of sport did not come naturally to writers, he regularly went around "dressed up as a sportsman,"[3] and he casually practiced fencing or shooting with a revolver. Last of all, he has baleful tastes. He adores owls because the masses shun them, goes in search of "arcane traditions, strange cases and unexplained facts,"[4] and though affecting to be a cynic, is a most considerate friend. Sinking ever deeper into solitude, when he dies in the Charité hospital, he appears "to have broken with all of his friends, including himself."[5] All of that links him to those literary schools for which literature is not everything, that—in appearance—prefer an everyday fact to a masterpiece, and, beneath an array of droll and rollicking activities, are seriously in search of poetic transcendence.

Jarry's importance is not limited to this gift for anticipation, however. He not only foresaw the habits and hopes of the young writers who would succeed him, he was himself a great writer, indeed almost a classical writer: a master of the language that he tormented, someone capable of the most natural poetry and the inventor of an image style from which his successors have benefitted. Take these lines from the *Supermale*, quoted by André Breton: "Her eyes . . . were so dark as to defy all color, like the dark, dead leaves at the bottom of the limpid Lourance moat, and they seemed like two wells in her skull, sunk for the joy of seeing her hair from the inside. . . . Her teeth were minute and well-kept toys. Death had carefully closed up the two rows, like tiny, unspotted dominoes—too childish for counting to matter—in a child's surprise box."[6] In the arrangement of the metaphors, in the development of similes that are superficially unjustifiable but establish themselves as they develop, discovering their own meaning as they progress toward other images, we find the main features of a form that Jean Giraudoux's *Provincial Ways* will inaugurate seven years later.[7] The impression of naturalness within virtuosity, of sensibility within artifice explains the extraordinary quality of *The Dragon Woman*, a posthumous novel by Jarry that his friend Jean Saltas has just published, preceded by a short introduction.[8] This is the last book on which the author of *King Ubu* was working; when he died, the first part was written, and from his sickbed he continued to dictate the notes needed to complete it to his sister. What we read is thus an unfinished book, but one that is more or less complete. It is not exactly unpublished, since fragments from it appeared during its author's lifetime in the *Revue Blanche* and *Vers et Prose*.

What is striking about this novel is the seriousness with which Jarry approached the writer's craft, developing a plot, working on character development, summoning up all manner of convincing characters against a background of caricature, not to mention sudden bursts of poetic imagination that disturb the order and make words the ultimate masters of the adventure. These two sides are not of equal interest. In the methodical narrative we encounter a calmer Jarry, very much at ease in a regular prose that he enlivens with puns and uses to convey his own pet obsessions, for example, his interest in provincial eccentricities, his anarchist's fondness for military discipline, and so forth. This produces some excellent gems, but basically, it never strays far from the world of Courteline. But suddenly, as if triggered by a device for pitching the writer of superficial comedy into a dangerously obscure fantasy, he surrounds himself with an imaginary world where, while remaining just as precise, logical and thorough, he assumes exorbitant powers over language and the mind. The description of what he calls the battle of Morsang will endure as an outstanding page of novel writing. We are shown a polytechnician—is it a dream, an inexplicable tear in the fabric of reality?—who uses his knowledge of military commands to lure regiments of soldiers who are quietly on maneuvers into a battle where they kill each other down to the last man. This scene could simply be no more than a rather horrible joke. But over and above the burlesque nature of the episodes, it uses the serious nature of the descriptions, the calculated placing of detail, and above all the power of the language to create an indefinable structural rigor and an inexorable certitude that allows the imagination no escape. There is nothing at all ponderous about these pages; they contain a dreamlike truth that reveals a possible future for humanity, as it destroys itself quietly and mathematically out of obedience to orders, wallowing gleefully in a parody of a massacre. At night, a battlefield can justify all sorts of confusion, but is clear that we are not dealing here with a simple misunderstanding that could be dispelled if it were explained: what happens is that one day, men hear the call of a desire, respond to it and are henceforth prey to a logic that is more powerful than any instinct, that deprives them of the capacity to be astonished at their absurd fate, or to feel despair. In this fable we can recognize some of the preoccupations of novel writing today. That alone is enough to remind us that Jarry remains our contemporary!

—April 13, 1944

Novellas and Stories

Claude Roy was bound to write excellent novellas. The art of the novella calls for something indefinably swift, a talent for allusion, a lightness of touch that does not make heavy weather of its discoveries, and feelings that are both veiled and embellished by fantasy. All of that is part of Claude Roy's world, with which we have become fondly familiar through his collections of poetry and his essay, *French Suite*.[1] These qualities are much rarer than would appear. Nothing is less easy than the ease to which we are given access. The least wrong move will place it under threat. Any overemphasis will alter it. A graceful style and a lively imagination will quickly repel us if they are not pure. And such purity is both the fruit of an original talent, and the result of a sustained effort to guard it from inconsistencies.

Claude Roy has a flair for the novella. His publisher advises us that we are not reading a truncated novel, or chapters taken from a novel. That is perfectly true. In each of the texts collected under the title *Asking the Impossible*,[2] it is a great pleasure to feel that the author has found his niche, that he has not had

The book that Marcel Béalu has just brought out with the title *Memories of Shadow* consists of very short pieces of one page or sometimes two.[3] This brevity is all the writer needs to express the world he sees, a world that is not exactly that of dream, but rather that of imaginary appearances beneath which the problems of real life become visible to us. For example, one of his prose pieces begins thus: "I had an important letter to write, a letter on which my entire life could well depend"; but this letter whose terms must be carefully weighed can never be written. During the day, time is taken up with this and that, and in the evening, the tired mind cannot bring itself to return to its task. "My life . . . just limped by, and I saw clearly that I would never manage to write that letter. Anyway, what was the point? I would sometimes say to myself, the person it is meant for must have been dead for ages." "Of course, I wouldn't have hurt a fly!" the narrator says in another story; however, on one occasion he does give one a swipe; a few moments later he sees it crawling across the floor, and it looks to him as if it has got bigger; he squashes it, but an enormous cockroach escapes from under his sole; he chases it and sees a monstrous black maybug crawling along, leaving a brownish smear . . . "Finally I managed to flatten it by stamping on it, leaving it motionless in a pool of blood. I turned round. All the members my family were seated around the table, looking at me with pained astonishment and a hint of reproach."

It is clear that Marcel Béalu uses images drawn from sleep, to put us in touch with the sense of an enigma that for some people provides the fundamental sense of their existence. It has become fashionable today to look for a precise view of human fate in the perspective offered by dream. What is strange is described precisely. What is bizarre is approached objectively, and with these visions that cannot be seen, the most ordinary level of life is lured into the trap of impossibility. (Inevitably, this will sooner or later give rise to stereotypes that are as hollow as the most threadbare devices of realism.) What gives

Memories of Shadow a quality that is not overshadowed by the works that they bring to mind is the extreme simplicity of their form. Their tone is calm; it does not try for effect, and it has no room for images. All it would take for their style to be truly effective is a greater degree of purity.

—April 20, 1944

Chateaubriand's Secret

In a lengthy, important study entitled *Chateaubriand, or The Obsession With Purity*,[1] Louis-Martin Chauffier goes in search of the inner significance to which Chateaubriand's life and work correspond. In his view, the extremely diverse tendencies of such a contradictory life all relate back to an identical attitude; they reflect not the division but the constancy of his nature, and by shedding light on the choice that was the fundamental choice in this life, he believes it possible to explain its specific and often elusive circumstances better than with the help of history and the testimony of the author's contemporaries. Chateaubriand has a secret that is in part a secret even for Chateaubriand. When he confides in people, he distorts it rather than revealing it. He conceals it out of a wish to appear the way he wants people to see him, and because he has a false view of himself. Nonetheless, it is in his work that we can most easily pursue this enigma, which, once it has been glimpsed, appears just as clearly in his political activity as in the episodes of his private emotional life. "Chateaubriand's sensibility," says

Martin-Chauffier, "is admirably monotonous. In whatever domain it is applied, it is always identical to itself. Chateaubriand the man of ambition is no different from Chateaubriand the lover."

This secret is not a simple one. The author of the *Genius of Christianity* is under a spell. He strives to possess everything with a powerful desire that few men have ever been capable of; he covets all things, and all things are granted him; but as soon as he takes hold of them, they turn to ashes in his hand; they become shadows, and he now considers their possession a paltry matter; his desire flags and dies, becomes disgust, then incurable ennui before soon reviving, thanks to hope of a new conquest that will make him just as eager to achieve it and just as disappointed and desperate as soon as he done so. As a result of this cruelly indirect form of sensibility, all he knows of people is a semblance of what they are. For as long as he remains aloof from them, he assumes their presence in his imagination, which stokes his passion by seducing it with fanciful images; then comes the moment of encounter, which is also what he turns away from, when, as he wrote to Léontine de Villeneuve, he has learned to "see the object of his illusions vanish at the very moment it reveals itself";[2] then, when it is all over, when death, ruin, and disaster have once again made inaccessible what he can only desire if it is absent, his passion, no longer afraid of being disappointed by reality, is inflamed yet again, achieves a moment of genuine happiness and endures unflaggingly, having ceased to fear that it will never be satisfied.

Though in many ways he is a realist who desires things in themselves and not the dream of them, Chateaubriand is nonetheless condemned to live in a universe where he sees nothing but mirages—mirages of the imagination when he anticipates the moment of possession, mirages of memory when he brings it back to life along with the past. He himself is perpetually deceived by these two alibis; he is present only for what is absent, and the more irrevocable the absence, the more faithful and captivated he is. It is therefore of no use to him to be given everything he longs for. He longed for glory, power, and love, and no one was more glorious, illustrious, and loved than he was. But these rewards come only in the form of what has ceased to be desirable; he possesses them in order to see how vain their possession is and yet begins to dread the day when he will be deprived of it. He wishes for life, life at its most concrete, Pauline, Juliette, Cordelia, honors, and the leadership of nations, yet he is only alive outside of life, face to face with himself; he conquers the universe, but it is in an imaginary world that he dwells, and he can only experience plenitude by feeling the emptiness of all that he touches, creating with all of this emptiness "a Paradise lost, where God himself is merely a ghost, where he alone exists and expresses himself, but does not know himself." Indeed, it is typical of Chateaubriand to find neither in his inner life nor in some absolute beyond anything that could satisfy him. His inner life is impoverished. When in 1831 he majestically goes into retirement, excluding himself from the century by exiling himself to Geneva, he quickly becomes alarmed by the silence he finds there. He sought the peace of solitude, and it offers him nothing; he is absent from himself the way he is absent from things, and he does not have the power to accept this pure vacancy, this hopeless bareness. As Martin-Chauffier quite rightly says: "Is it possible to imagine a life more constantly haunted by unhappiness, yet more untouched by true anguish?" If his faith is firm and guarantees him a degree of intellectual security, it is entirely separate from what he is in search of, and that can satisfy him solely because it is vain. God is not what he lacks; what he lacks is what he has. He is entirely turned outward and not inward; he wants the fruits of the earth rather than spiritual happiness, but as soon as he possesses them, the things he nonetheless wished for are no more than surface appearance for which he feels disdain, and he dreams of a truer essence, expressed through death that purifies all.

Existence could have been more absurd for Chateaubriand had he not been able to enjoy it in the past, recapture it through memory, and finally give it the meaning he could not find in life by changing it into a work of art. That is why no writer has given his memoirs the importance that the *Memoirs from Beyond the Tomb* held for Chateaubriand. Not only did he work at them for over thirty years, devoting most of his literary energies to them, seeking consolations from them that life can only provide in the form of disappointments, but he prepared them as if they were his own rebirth, like the second life that follows death, and that is the only thing that can illuminate people in his eyes, and through its purity at last make them commensurate with his desires. In a whole range of telling phrases, Martin-Chauffier explains the decisive role that the *Memoirs* played in a life that they saved from being meaningless. The *Memoirs from Beyond the Tomb* first allow Chateaubriand to depict the fate of a man who keeps his fantasies in check without ever resisting their allure. They then allow him to shed light on what he was, by revealing what he finds remarkable about himself: "an extraordinary sensibility and the most magnificently unhappy man who ever walked the earth." They give him the means to live again in the strongest sense of the term, to live again because he begins his life by recounting it, but even more because he recounts it not as he lived it but as he rediscovered it in the enchantment of his memory, with the melancholic fullness of what can no longer be either lost or retrieved. The past has the purity of dreams, and their absolute nature. If Chateaubriand can write that, like "the girls of his imagination . . . the realities of his days 'have' themselves the allure of fantasies," it is because he looks at them through a thick layer of duration, in that flow of time that makes them beautiful by being their ruin. The *Memoirs* provide him with a permanent dialogue between a past reality that he regrets, but that is transfigured by regret, and the present that in comparison with days gone by appears derisory but is enriched by them through that comparison. With the years, the role played by the *Memoirs* becomes prodigious. Destined initially to allow him to begin his life again, they soon become its double and then eventually replace it. Through the intervention of the narrator, the man becomes a hero, but the hero eventually gives way to the narrator, and all that matters is the narrative, which, having reconstituted the life so as to give it the perfection of a work, replaces it with the masterpiece for which life is merely the occasion. It is thus quite superfluous to ask about sincerity or truth. The past is not what has been already lived, but a great empty space that he organizes to accommodate his dreams, and into which, under the cloak of the memories that he evokes, he transposes the feelings he experiences in the process of describing those memories. And since Chateaubriand does not change, since he was never able to find reasons in an experience for preventing himself from reliving it, and since few temperaments were as impermeable and as unvarying as his, he is basically accurate when he merges the feelings of the actor with those of the author and describes a strange destiny without progress, without development, and without pause, that bears the burden at every moment of the same innocence and the same commitment to unhappiness.

—April 27, 1944

Fantastic Novels

It is the exodus. A young woman from Liège finds herself drawn into dark and derisory adventures whose conventions have been established by an abundance of literary works. Bombings, tank battles, soldiers in combat mixed up with fleeing evacuees, frantic rushing along roads, persistent encounters between people who have never met, friends who are separated, death so present it has become invisible, everyday concerns that still survive mingled with exorbitant feelings, and then the growing impression that anything now is possible, that laws govern nothing but what deviates from them, in a closed world where people have been imprisoned by accident. In this tumult of insignificant and extraordinary events, the young woman continues on her way, unmoved by the events she encounters. Where does the extraordinary begin and experience end? That is a question that the mind tends not to ask itself. From time to time, unexpected physical phenomena intrude on the workings of the absurd machine: for example, in some areas veritable hordes of caterpillars appear, or else water becomes no more than a horrible, almost living substance, or else a vapor spreads through the air and takes hold of the soul, making it kind and delirious with tenderness and devotion. Soon these phenomena become more persistent. The heroine meets someone who reveals something to her about her fate. She is aware that what is taking place is the war, but that it is also something more than the war. Beneath what appear as intelligible catastrophes she glimpses the unleashing of infernal forces. She realizes that time is coming to an end and that deep in people's hearts, fearful and admirable secrets are being unleashed. Then there begins a carnival of mysteries: giant moles, innumerable serpents, blood that runs pale, the dead who take on the appearance of animals, all of this sorcery shows that the war is no more than a tiny catastrophe, lost among the preparations for a universal disaster. "It's a good thing I left," the heroine says to herself, "and left for good." For here now are the last signs that are a prelude to the coming of the Spirit.

Robert Poulet has written a very able book on this theme, and one that is extremely interesting, although all told it falls short of its own ambitions.[1] It does not so much offend against verisimilitude as against a deeper sense that concerns the value of events. The reader willingly moves between the real and the fantastic, but what does he gain? The abnormal episodes are weak in comparison with the actual facts that imagination supposes or memory recalls. There is nothing less alarming than imaginary visions; they possess neither obscure significance nor seductive power; they entertain more than they scare; they are simply ingenious whimsy, appearing mediocre and almost shocking in the wake of tragic historical catastrophes. There are two things that Robert Poulet can be reproached for. His description of the exodus is lively, the writing has excellent pace, but it does not rise above the level of talented reporting. The real events that he describes have no density, or even any reality: We do not doubt them, because we know very well that they did generally happen that way, but we feel lukewarm about them, the way we would feel about a story that conformed to cliché, without appealing to our capacity to live and die. This war reporting is followed by the reporting of supernatural events. But far from offering a profound insight into human ills, these events are no match for the upheavals that they seek to upstage. Compared to the war, apocalypse has something faintly banal about it, and this detracts considerably from the state of panic into which the author tries to plunge us. Caterpillars, serpents, and fantastic horses are all prophetic apparitions that frighten us neither by the way they look nor by the memories they recall. We remain free. Our minds are no more in thrall to dream than they are to reality.

Robert Poulet was perhaps wrong to take as the point of departure for his tale of wonders a set of circumstances that literature can for the moment neither express directly nor distort. The fact is that of all the stories relating to the contemporary world, the only ones that are acceptable are remote fictions such as Noël Devaulx's *Mystical Wine-Press*,[2] that transpose into a universe with neither date nor reference point, the meaning of events that are recognizable beneath their tragic disguise. *Prelude to Apocalypse* appears unfaithful when it is no more than a documentary, and inadequate when it makes a historical accident function as the lead-up to the end of the world. It expresses what is strange about war neither when it tells it as it is nor when it dresses it up as something fantastic: There is something missing, namely the specific nature of the human condition. The main interest of the book lies in the movement that drives the reader from a world he knows, or thinks he knows, into a world that he cannot accept. This transition takes place thanks to a very skillful story. The narrative is so lively that it absorbs our attention and does with it as it pleases. The author's sole accomplice is the reader, whom he carries with him not by means of anguish or some profound truth but through his intense interest in what he is reading.

The scientific-marvelous novel is a dangerous genre that has tempted some great writers, and given rise to some well-known works. Edgar Allan Poe created the mold, and his two tales, water, slow-moving water, stagnant water, the material substrate of death, the expression of an interminable descent into oblivion and nothingness.

With *Air and Dreams*, Bachelard pursues his examination, but more thoroughly, enriching it with literary and philosophical ambitions that make it more substantial and a little less clear. Several chapters are devoted to an examination of the airy imagination. To be sensitive to air is in fact to be sensitive to movement in the air, conscious of an alleviation, a liveliness, a lightness. If we explore dream for an experience that every dreamer has had, namely flying, the indelible impression of taking to the air, of a freely gliding movement, of joyful confident uplift, we discover in it the source of numerous images destined for use in poetry. Thus Shelley is in harmony with the air, and his poetry is a veritable dream flight, that rises gently and becomes a calm, ascending light. Nietzsche is also an airy mind ("Storm clouds, what matter it what you are? To us free spirits, airy spirits, joyous spirits.");[2] his imagination is upward movement, conquest of the cold and silent air of the peaks; flight is a judgment that condemns the inertia and ponderousness of the world ("Whoever one day teaches humans to fly will have shifted all boundary-stones; for him, all boundary-stones themselves will fly into the air; he will christen the earth anew as 'the light one'").[3]

Gaston Bachelard studies the poetic images that the airy imagination projects onto the blue sky, the constellations, the clouds, and the Milky Way. He sketches the broad outlines of a poetics of storm, of violent air and angry winds. Then, taking literally the expression the breath of poetic inspiration (*le souffle poétique*), he identifies in it an actual reality—not just a simple metaphor—that gives life to the poem and that the reader must seek to recapture. The verse line is under the influence of the airy imagination; it is a breathing silence, the freedom of a tacit voice, the vocal dream of breath. Silent declamation is the principle of all poetry. In these studies, with a richness of interpretation and a gift for language that are truly exceptional,

Bachelard expresses a conception of the imagination, or more precisely of the imaginative life, whose literary and philosophical consequences he also describes. For him, man is first and foremost a dream; he is imaginative power before he is sensibility and reason. Human beings imagine the world they do not know; they experience wonder, and this wonder is their dream. Then they contemplate, and their contemplation revives their dreams, organizes them, and displays them as poetic knowledge. Reasoned knowledge that employs forms and explains the world only comes at the end. What is primordial in humans is the movement of dream; man the dreamer, dreaming man who is indifferent to objects that have shape, but sensitive to something more elementary that is vested in image, is the expression of mankind when it is truly free, the veritable key to mankind.

What makes Bachelard's thought somewhat questionable is the fact that it develops on several levels and combines claims or discoveries that are distinct. The first theme relates to the existence within things, beyond the visual forms that generally attract attention, of material meanings to which human dreams instinctively attach themselves. The fluid, the igneous, the compact, and the airy are elemental qualities whose significance can be explored, and that affect artistic sensibility more profoundly than external forms or appearances. The critic must pay attention to these deep layers, these primordial sites in which the tendency to dream, and especially to write down one's dreams, is based. This angle of approach restores works to their true perspective, and does not only enrich our capacity to explain them, but more importantly, increases our capacity to admire them and be sensitive to them. But Bachelard accompanies this with a theory of imagination that remains confused. What are image and imagination for him? That is not clear. He readily emphasizes the predominance of dream, of the imaginative powers, in short—in keeping with the great Romantic tradition—the preeminence of the imaginary. Nothing could be more congenial from a literary point of view than this position, but the question remains: what is it based on and what does it mean? Bachelard appears never to provide a precise definition of the term image, nor to examine the classic problem of the relations between "perception" and "imagination." Sometimes, he appears to rely on a vaguely Bergsonian approach, that turns out in this case to be far from coherent. He is firmly opposed to realism and content to focus on certain characteristics such as the spontaneity, the living movement, or the impulsive nature of image, even though they are insufficient in themselves to distinguish images from things. On the other hand, when he defends the primacy of the imagination, he sees in man first and foremost the power to go beyond the real, to negate it in order to be free, to produce an unreality whose mode of existence is absolutely original; and this ought to allow him to claim, in opposition to Bergson, that if image is in no way a copy of a thing, a thing is no more an immobile depository for images.

From the standpoint of poetic and literary aesthetics, Bachelard derives some highly interesting views from his thinking about images. For him, the literary image cannot naturally constitute the outer garb of an idea. It is not even a metaphor or a symbol, in the sense of a figure referring to a reality that would otherwise remain inexpressible. The literary image is primordial. It is poetry itself; there is no poetry, no poetic mystery or truth prior to the image that presents it to us. To ask if there is within us a poetry that exists before words, before images, a poetic precondition, a blank and a silence that language seeks to reproduce, is to misunderstand literary activity, which is a natural, original activity corresponding to the direct action of the imagination—the faculty for producing unreality that constitutes consciousness itself—on language. The imagination naturally takes the form of speech. It is wrong to say that it awakens silent voices; in fulfilling itself in the form of written sounds, it restores them to dream and to the speechlessness out of which they arise. It is thus that image is linked to writing; it is the birth of significance, of a new meaning that in its turn is the call of a dream of which the written word becomes conscious. To write is of necessity to give material form to an imaginary world. "What the writer had intended to say is so quickly replaced by what he discovers himself writing that he feels clearly that the written language is creating its own universe. A universe of sentences arranges itself on the blank page with a coherence of image that often obeys very diverse laws, but which always observes the great laws of the imaginary. . . . The most revolutionary manifestoes . . . may cause us to change universes, but they always shelter us in an imaginary one."[4] Nothing more apt could possibly be said in our view about the meaning and creative capacity of literary language.

—May 11, 1944

Joyce's First Novel

It is a strange fact that while Joyce's first novel can be read effortlessly and is filled with accessible literary delights, it is much less well known than *Ulysses*, not to mention *Finnegans Wake*, whose merits can be appreciated by only a few people today. *A Portrait of the Artist as a Young Man* has vanished behind the unparalleled celebrity of these extraordinary works. Less visibly original, and similar in appearance to other novels, it has been neglected in favor of extreme books that it would in fact have served to make more comprehensible. It has been customary to see it as the work of a novice, one that according to Louis Gillet in *Claybook for James Joyce*, "while unprecedentedly bold for England, broke no mold."[1] It has been seen as a preparatory work, necessary for its author but offering nothing to the public. What is more, having been published in less than ideal circumstances, at least in France, it soon became impossible to find. Consequently, this latest publication, in an excellent translation by Ludmila Savitzky, will reveal it a wider public.[2]

The fact is, however, that it is impossible to read *Portrait* as the work of just any author. It appeals because of its refinement, the way it develops and explores its subject and the beauty of a style that is both very subtle and very sensitive. But it is to Joyce that we continually return in this self-portrait or autobiography, that shows his life to be the source all of the great themes that his later works will interpret, with a brilliance of invention for which there have been few equivalents in all of literature. *Portrait* is the story of Joyce, of Joyce's youth, of the vocation he became aware of, and furthermore, as Ludmila Savitzky remarks, it is a magical portrait. A magical portrait creates the being it reveals. It endows ordinary events with unique and exemplary significance. It describes actual circumstances not for their historical truth but for the myths they reveal. Behind everyday incidents a figure can be seen taking shape solely through the radiant significance it possesses. We do not witness the formation of a character; character traits are the passing expression of events that are of a universal nature, timeless motifs that coincide with an individual life; they resemble the figures that the constellations form in the sky, and that before they are forms are a twinkling streak of light, a fiery system.

The beginning of *Ulysses* follows on from *Portrait*. Stephen Dedalus is the same person whom we discover in the closing pages of the biography. He is the artist he wished to become. The word artist is full of amphibologies and shifting meanings, as are most of the terms Joyce uses, and it is one of the keywords in the work. It is not only an allusion to the writer whose portrait it defines, but it also indicates the ideal he sought for and the slow process during which he took possession of it. The artist has nothing in common with the simple, brilliant colors in which the everyday world depicts him. The conquest of art is the conquest of the absolute. It is the negation of the traditional world, the assertion of a freedom that can tolerate no limits, and the expression of an individual life in terms of the privileges that are indispensable to it. It refers not to a technique but to a vision of the world, and to the life that this vision presupposes.

second, everything is energy, the indefinite renewal of language, expressive virtuosity, and the sovereign creation of meaning through words. Nonetheless, the transition from one to the other happens naturally. Joyce's great works are immense dreams that use the whole of reality to reveal their enigmas, and *Portrait* is a discreet reverie, full of charm and intensity, that wraps itself around the events of a life and expresses their universal significance.

—May 18, 1944

A Secret Tone

First cubism, then surrealism, have taught us to see in the most banal objects an allusion to a strange world. And great artists have no doubt been capable in every era of freeing things from the everyday purblindness that obscures their image. They have offered them to a disinterested gaze. They have turned them into still lives, that is, into objects that can no longer be put to use and that, now redundant, are truly "offered to our gaze" (*donnés à voir*).[1] However, this aesthetic contemplation is very different from what surrealism went in search of. The surrealists required everyday reality to provide them with forms that were more marvelous than the most outlandish dreams. In certain lights and from certain perspectives, they transformed the real into the imaginary. They revealed to us that the world we live in is as enigmatic, as terrible, and as abnormal as the universe of our dreams and nightmares. There is no continuity between the real and the surreal. Lautréamont's famous phrase "As beautiful as the encounter, on a dissecting table, between a sewing-machine and an umbrella" became a key phrase for the surrealists because it gives preeminence to objects that are ugly and without formal value; and yet for the mind—if not for the eye—what it derives from their encounter is a surprise, something exciting, something secretly extraordinary.

Marcel Lecomte's book *A Secret Tone* is not unrelated to these concerns, but it is so discreet that it is from within (as though they were turned inwards) and without the least wish to cause astonishment, that he captures the astounding images that the attentive gaze borrows momentarily from ordinary life, in order to penetrate the heart of their silent existence or their poetic vigor.[2] This little book takes us into the street or into cafés; it shows us what we are used to seeing; it describes incidents that are a part of our experience: the stranger we bump into every day, in the same spot, the young woman we see through her window, combing her hair in front of a mirror, or the cry that we hear. Nothing could be more usual or less selective. Furthermore, the author describes what he sees without transforming it through image; metaphors are few in number, and we are not disconcerted by unexpected combinations of words. It is this discretion and this silence that partly give us the impression that we are making an authentic discovery as we read some of these pages. There is no trickery, no contrivance. If there is something indefinably secret about the spectacle of everyday life, it is through stealth, by approaching it tentatively and thoughtfully with a sort of phlegmatic attentiveness, and above all by making space in our souls that we have a chance of glimpsing it, paying attention less to things than to their profiles, less to voices than to their tone and to those mysterious resonances that can only be properly heard if we keep silent.

In one of his tableaux, Marcel Lecomte describes a young man whose eyes, he says, "had a truly moving brightness whenever they entered the light, and attached themselves persistently to the object of their attention, very quickly surrounding it with a sort of solitude." This attitude puts him in touch with the sensual truth of things. The word "sensual" (*sensible*) recurs frequently in his writing. "I acquired a sort of strange freedom through having perceived some of those highly sensual moments in life that scarcely allowed themselves to be expressed." Or else: "So what is it about the humblest objects in our bedrooms, in the least solemn curves of their outline, or about the dark recesses of some of the protruding parts of our most familiar items of furniture, that make them seem so sensual to look at?" In fact, "sensual" is a two-pronged term, an ambiguous word that is both active and passive and that functions in both the inner and the outer world: A sensual object presents itself in a special way to our senses, but in itself it has a sentimental quality at the same time: it possesses a particular warmth and delicacy that we share in: it is not only a stone or a tree, it is also sensual, and this sensuality that our everyday lives take no account of is the secret that is revealed at propitious moments, the revelation that, without changing its meaning or its form, transfigures the real or more precisely, releases it from its slumber.

We do not see things, nothing could be more certain. But seeing is an immeasurably delicate process. Attention is not enough, we must impose a degree of solitude on what we look at, we must alter the rhythm of our vision, and through our slow and drowsy assent, seize hold of the novelty that eludes too lucid a gaze. "This landscape does not reveal itself to everyone," writes Marcel Lecomte. "It calls for slow reading." Several of his best encounters are masterpieces of slow contemplation: the simplest gesture, decomposed through minute observation, becomes a figure whose presence is disturbing; it is no longer a movement, it is an apparition, a form detached from its purpose, a pure fragment, available to be enjoyed immediately and bathed in the radiance of a denser, deeper life. Through this change of rhythm, relations between people are deepened. The sea and the sun become elements in a meditation that culminates in a sort of spiritual rapture. The landscape is attentive only to itself; it is its own reflection and is in harmony with itself; it is anticipation, interruption and manifestation; it emerges slowly from a dream.

"This moment was particularly rich. My perception of it was overwhelming in the sense that it filled me with the sensation of watching myself participate in the true course of things. The true course, thanks to the unexpected." And indeed, the unexpected is not there so as to disrupt the natural order of images, but solely so as to make it visible. It is a signal that directs our gaze toward "the extraordinarily strange and everyday appearance of a body, a gesture, an arm tracing a pattern through space, of feet stepping one after another over stones."

This solitary, silent vision, the reverie of a discreet spectator, does not only restore the "immediate life" or what is most sensual in life to him, it hints at its ceremonial character. When we separate actions from their practical significance, some attitudes appear to correspond to a ritual. They suggest conventions that we do not understand and yet appear magical to us, that repeat themselves inexhaustibly and express themselves faithfully. Thanks to the ceremonies they perform, the most mundane acts give us back a sense of our relations with ourselves. They bring us back to what we are, and convey to us what we desire. They are like a language that, amid the dissipation and absence of each day, reasserts the possibility of understanding, agreement, and mysteriously preestablished harmony. We happened one day to dream of a town through which we wandered without recognizing it. There was no lack of familiar landmarks, but we were looking for exact indications capable of situating us in our dream, and putting an end to our drifting. Here is the outcome that Marcel Lecomte gives to that dream: "Suddenly the brilliant sky dazzled me, then in a split second my own name appeared on a sign at the corner of a street! And I had just enough time to recognize the town, yes, I recognized it, yet without finding it possible or necessary to name it, for I realized then that it had never stopped being a sort of language that I had invented in order to establish contact with myself."

It is that language that Marcel Lecomte, the new "solitary wanderer," teaches us to perceive. It is both a ritual and a sensual movement, a convention and an instinctive image. It is a silent language, totally inward, seeming audible only to itself. It allows the individual to attain a creative tone, and allows him to see in things either the expression of a secret or the secret of expression, as he sees fit.

—May 25, 1944

works refer to him only indirectly, either as Théophile or as M. Godeau, and contain all of the mythic variety that an impersonal story allows, in his more recent books, whether it be *On Abjection* or *Marital Chronicles*, the short narrative he has entitled *My Own* or the latest one to appear, *Uncle Henry*, it is he himself and all his family, without the semblance of a fable or the screen of a pseudonym, that are portrayed in a form that could not be more direct, and more remote from the usual literary precautions.[2] As for the meaning of such a change, it would be rather risky to seek to discover it. The writer would appear to have gradually abandoned his myths, not because of the transfigurations they permitted but from a greater and perhaps purer desire to discover himself: He has left them behind the way one rejects alibis, those alibis that are all the more reliable for being intimately close to you and that entail tangled involvements and infinite resemblances. Having observed himself in a double who imitated every aspect of him, and who was only different from him because it was more him than he could ever be, he has come back to himself, fallen back on himself (for the moment at least), at last examining and expressing that rarest and most inaccessible of all witnesses, without any intermediary. M. Godeau was initially more real than the writer; today it is the writer who is more symbolic than his character.

It is possible to argue therefore—to the extent that such brutal expressions can convey something true—that having started by writing works in which he concealed himself in order to describe himself, if he has now turned to narratives that have no pretext, it is because in himself he has gone from a subjective stage to an objective stage, and because the *I* that he is currently revealing with such simplicity and frankness is both more immediate and more reflective, and also better adapted to literary transposition than the characters in the early works. The same can no doubt be said for those whom Jouhandeau calls *My Own*. At first, he could only see them through the pseudonymous heroes who revealed their truth and their existence, in the fabulous town of Chaminadour that was nonetheless identical to his birthplace, Guéret, where their destinies were decided; but today he has rediscovered them, indeed reincarnated them in their own lives, and without adding any borrowed features to either their appearance or their history, he represents them in an admirable light, in the dark and dazzling splendor that illuminates the finest imaginary figures.

The triptych he has assembled under the title *Uncle Henry* is thus a threefold portrait of his family, that at the same time provides three new variations on his favorite theme: the equivalence between abjection and glory, the dignity that the soul that has fallen into the pit derives from its fidelity to pride. Something like a halo, a sort of violent radiance, or impassioned light, or imperious sunburst that no shadow can darken, not even that of imminent death, surrounds Uncle Henri, a splendid Don Juan who has lived like a king and who eventually sinks into the most wretched poverty, yet who, having plumbed these depths, maintains an ostentatiousness, a capacity to be himself and to deny himself, a radiant impulsiveness; it also surrounds Aunt Marguerite, who ends up in the poorhouse, and dies a humiliating death covered in vermin and filth; and finally their son, the writer's godson, little Jean. Little Jean lives in a hovel with his cantankerous mother and is the victim of endless cruelties. One day, when he is twelve years old, he steals a coin from money that belongs to his school. Abandoned by his mother, who puts him into juvenile detention, he is visited in jail by his affectionate godfather, who does not reproach him but eventually says to him: "dear little Jean, you know that I forgive you of course, but at least tell me it's over, and that you won't cause me the same upset again." But to retract, to deny something that is a part of you, even if it is a crime, is something that the pride of this indomitable breed cannot accept . . . "When I embraced him, he did not return my embrace, he looked stern, and was determined to punish me as much as he was able, while perhaps regretting that he could not rebuke me on the spot for my impertinence. His dignified manner and expression suddenly reminded me that I should respect the little fellow, as if in his mind he had brought a case of *lèse-majesté* against me at the same moment, so much so that, had I turned up the following day, he would have refused to see me."

The writer is not absent from any of these three episodes. Not only are they about his uncle, his aunt, and his godson; through unexpected encounters and as though he were charged with a task by some dark Providence from which he is indistinguishable, a sounder-out of abysmal tragedies and a provoker of the absolute, it is also he who delivers up to their infernal fate souls that are as remote as possible from each other, entirely absent and entirely unthroned. That is what makes him a miracle worker who can write: "Do I ask myself if I believe in miracles! I say to myself I have seen them, I have worked them." His memories do not relate to any particular life. They are memorable anecdotes, confidences whispered in an ear that retains nothing of the world save what is glorious and secret about it.

—June 1, 1944

Charles Cros

Once again, it is the surrealists we have to thank for granting Charles Cros the status he deserves. They sensed that this rarest of minds, whose discretion was exemplary and who seemed to conspire in his own misfortune, bore a great name that remained hidden from sight. They understood that for French schools of poetry he would always remain an outsider, a poet whose delicacy, appetite for renewal and above all, disturbing simplicity, made him indifferent to all of the homage that people sought to bestow on him. He is one of those unclassifiable spirits who in France make up the tradition of those who defy tradition. It is hard to know what to say about them: misunderstood yet appreciated at their true value, liked for being unusual and so liked that they earn universal fame; peremptorily promoted by some, but for reasons in which they basically fail to recognize themselves. In any case, there was a pressing need to collect together Charles Cros's works, and much gratitude is owed to Henri Parisot for a producing a perfect edition that presents them to us in a form with which we are not familiar: poems, fantasies in verse and prose, along with scientific writings, preceded by an introduction by Maurice Saillet whose subtle commentary is like a whispered clarification.[1]

Charles Cros was a contemporary of the symbolists. He was a friend of Verlaine's, and briefly a companion of Rimbaud's. In the "Hydropaths" club he became the intimate friend of Alphonse Allais. His life is so exceptionally devoid of anecdote that it conceals him from us, as if his delicacy had called for a dormant existence from which his sociability and the role he played in literary cabarets were as incapable of rousing him as his works were. These achieved only modest fame. *The Sandalwood Casket* attracted a few select readers, foremost among whom seems to have been Félix Fénéon, himself a writer almost without readers.[2] *The Necklace of Claws* is a posthumous work that was published thanks to the devotion of Renée Vivien.[3] Benefiting from the eagerness that precursors always inspire after the event, and even more so from national pride, the scientific work was defended and recognized more quickly. It is reasonably well known nowadays that several months before Edison, Charles Cros invented the phonograph, which he named the "paleophone" (the voice of the past), and that he was the first to demonstrate the principle of color photography, to propose the artificial synthesis of precious stones and finally to imagine a number of experiments that were subsequently put into practice by foreign scientists.

Charles Cros's poetry may strike the inattentive ear by the resemblances it displays. Quite often, it yields lazily to Baudelaire's influence. But in fact, it is highly individual. It is strange—almost foreign, so receptive is it to simplicity. It is simple in word, theme, and melody; it sings unaffectedly and is utterly without pretense; it is humble and clear; it offers itself for what it is. But strangely, this simplicity looks as though it has been invented, or rather not invented but chanced upon. Such an encounter is typical of this poet; the simplicity he finds excludes both experimentation and naivety, the effort of a thinking mind and the effort of distraction; it is a candor that catches

ideal rapidly leveled things down, there still remained the memory of the three original tribes, the "Tities," the "Ramnes," and the "Luceres," whose unification is said to have given rise originally to the power of the city, but these tribes call to mind ethnic elements rather than specific social functions. Indeed, we know that the Ramnes were the companions of Romulus and Remus, and they were joined after a war by the Sabines of King Titus Tatius (the Tities), and were assisted, in the same war, by the Etruscan armed forces of Lucumo (the Luceres).

Dumézil has shown that this ethnic conception of the early tribes was perfectly compatible with the functional explanation implied by the Indo-Iranian analogy. During the reign of Augustus, as both Virgil's texts and above all Propertius's elegy *De Urbe Roma* confirm, a deep-rooted tradition still claimed that "Remus and his brother," that is, the Ramnes, were not only the Albani, but also the custodians of religious and political administration; that as well as providing the Sabine contribution, the Tities were the group that specialized in cattle-raising and agriculture; and last that the Luceres or Etruscans were preeminently warriors. These accounts, when interpreted properly, thus restore to us a complete image of early Rome as the comparison with other, more easily traceable Indo-European groups allows us to understand it. Furthermore, it is possible to grasp why, in this tableau of origins, an ethnic idea was associated with a functional idea, why the history of three races gradually replaced the memory of the three functions. Among the other Indo-European peoples, we find myths that give equal status to the two explanations. Among the Scandinavian tribes, for example, the war between the gods of the Ases and the gods of the Vanes is the exact replica in heaven of the war between the Romans and the Sabines: In each case, two hostile races wage a war with no outcome, after which the adversaries are reconciled, exchange hostages, and sign advantageous treaties. The same pattern is found in Irish and Indian folklore. On the basis of this detailed comparison and the examination of numerous similar facts, Dumézil concludes that early Roman history is almost entirely mythical. Whenever we think we a dealing with unique facts that express an original historical development, we are actually dealing not only with contrived elements drawn from legend, but with fables belonging to the common store of the Indo-European domain, fables that explain in almost the same way, for every people, through what mechanisms they came into being and developed.

Georges Dumézil devotes one of the most important chapters of his book to the relations between history and myth in the narratives of ancient Rome. If there are so many mythical elements to be found in the legend of Rome's origins, how can their interpretation be reconciled with the perspectives with which historians have familiarized us? This reconciliation must be more or less abandoned. We know nothing about the facts that lie behind the classical narratives. Romulus, Numa, and Tullus are names that correspond much more to symbolic events than to real people. It is ancestral mythology that provided the opposing characteristics and attributes of the first two kings of Rome. The wolf-king (*roi-Lupesque*) Romulus, who is semidivine, capricious, and formidable, contrasts with the priest-king Numa. Similarly, the episode of Horace and the Curiaces is not a fact that has been more or less distorted, and that really did exemplify the early period of royal Rome. It is the dramatization, in moral and human terms, of a myth that underpinned the initiation rites of young warriors among the Western Indo-Europeans. Last, it is difficult to consider the war between the Romans and the Sabines as historical fact, since it reproduces, down to the smallest detail, a number of legends designed to explain the union between conquerors and natives and the creation of a stable society. Dumézil subjects the social existence of the Sabine people to detailed scrutiny. In particular, he rejects André Piganiol's claim that this people indisputably has a non-Indo-European origin, specifically an Illyrian one, and that they were active from the earliest days of Rome. In fact it is likely that the Sabines did not contribute the Mediterranean component to the common heritage, as they are said to have done; they belong to the same civilization as their cousins from Latium, and it is likely that they appeared too late on the site of Rome to have been able to play a decisive role in its foundation.

How did this early history in which everything is fable, expressive legend, or anachronistic fake come into being? Whence comes the tissue of events and episodes that turns this protohistory into a detailed romance that is admirably narrated and full of psychological appeal? First of all, says Dumézil, from later Roman history. That is Theodor Mommsen's well-known claim. Following the developments that almost entirely erased the early social structures, the Romans forgot their origins and constructed others for themselves by aging their experiences and those of their recent ancestors. Hence, according to Mommsen, the rape of the Sabine women and the war between Romulus and Tatius prefigure the historic third-century pact through which Rome effectively allied itself with the totality of the Sabine peoples. The annalists propose a first legendary version of the historical event, by utilizing more recent facts along with mythic structures that foreshadowed, at the dawn of time, a history that was more or less analogous with that of two peoples becoming reconciled after a long war, and uniting through a series of marriages for the greater common glory. Anachronism would clearly not suffice to explain the narratives proposed by the annalists. Their very substance is drawn from mythological memory, from the stock of legends, institutions and ancestral images preserved by popular tradition and the religious authorities. An epic of origins existed before Rome itself did. It is not unique to this people, since something similar can be found in other sectors of Indo-European civilization. What defines it is its moral, human character, its psychological awareness, the ideal of civic dignity and rigor that constitutes the infusion of the spirit of republican Rome into the era of fable.

It is not possible in these brief notes to examine the scope and significance of Dumézil's important conclusions. He can never hope to win over entirely to his cause those historians who will always be reluctant to explain precise events with the aid of an appealing mix of legend and speculation. What we see competing in these models is a dual type of truth. The people that came to settle on the Cermalus Hill brought with it an "early history," an origin myth that explained how it came into being. That is the myth that was made historical through the conscious invention of names and subsequent facts, and it is what prevailed over the real events that marked the first years of Rome. But this myth itself was probably true, having often become a reality during previous ancestral migrations. It expresses what generally took place between groups of conquerors and native peoples: a long war followed by reconciliation, then marriages. It proposes a sort of law or legal explanation of events, in relation to which aberrations and exceptions have no claim to represent the truth. Similarly, what is important in early history is not the positive reality of the narratives, their raw truth, the uniquely essential fact, but much rather the symbolic, moral, or religious significance that each event and each character bears. Every event has a meaning that is sufficient to make it true. Every conflict points to a religious or institutional notion that represents its permanent reality. "We will only fully understand this pseudo-history," says Dumézil, "when we have fully accepted the idea that it is philosophy expressed as drama." It is in this sense that we may say of this pseudo-history (as it were playfully, and in an anti-Hegelian spirit), that it is more genuinely Hegelian than history in the strict sense.

—June 15, 1944

William Blake

The *Selected Poems* of William Blake have been brought together and most ingeniously and skillfully translated by Madeleine L. Cazamian, who has also written a very full introduction to this edition.[1] They will undoubtedly encourage a better understanding of this great poet. No modern literature can boast a freer spirit, or one who is at the same time more devoted to his mission, a poetic genius who is more bountiful, more refined, and more faithful to his inner visions, or a man more hostile to all religion yet more tormented by his mystical tendencies. His great poems recall the mythological systems of the pre-Socratics or the great Hindu theogonies. They display the same prodigious inventiveness and imaginative power, and the same hidden significance. But Blake is a contemporary of the French Revolution. If his works have the authority of the great impersonal works that appear to be the products of archaic popular tradition, they wrestle with their times, not so as to hang back from them but to be ahead of them. They are inspired by a spirit of freedom that continues to deserve our interest and our attention. They reflect a moral imagination in revolt with which we continue to be in sympathy.

The problems raised by such a poetic genius are innumerable. One of those we shall explore concerns the intimate fusion of thought and image, meaning and imagination, that gives his work its originality. "Allegory address'd to the Intellectual powers, while it is altogether hidden from the Corporeal Understanding, is my Definition of the most Sublime Poetry,"[2] as he himself wrote. The terms of this definition were not chosen at random. They correspond to ideas that he defended throughout his life, and that are linked to his awareness of his prophetic destiny. It is W. B. Yeats who said: "Blake is a literalist of the imagination."[3] He follows his imagination to the letter. He has visions, and he obeys his visions. As a child he had seen angels in the branches of trees; later, partly influenced by Swedenborg, he was constantly in conversation with the prophets and the illustrious dead, with angels and demons. He often claimed that his books were dictated to him by spirits: They would wake him in the night, and he would get up and write, sometimes for hours, never allowing himself to make any change to what they confided in him.

But if Blake is a visionary, and if this term must be understood in the strict sense, nonetheless his apparitions do not in themselves display a brutal reality that would eliminate their significant value. First of all, most of them are subjective in origin. When he was asked one day where he saw everything he reported, he replied, "Here," and struck his forehead. At the same time, he does not believe in the supernatural. What he sees belongs to this world. It is the world itself, freed from the errors and the lies that our limited senses make us take for reality, whereas they are just superficial illusions, truth in a fallen state. We must look, he proclaims, "with, not through, the eye,"[4] and no more consult our vision than we would a window about the object that we see through it. Where others see a thistle, he recognizes a white-haired old man, and the sun is not a disk as yellow as a guinea, it is an angelic host singing Hosanna. Such remarks show clearly that many of Blake's visions are first and foremost metaphors: immediate fictions whose meaning and appearance are visited on him, but that also have an immediate meaning, that reveal something, and closely link a form to a language. For Blake, the real things that we see must give way to imaginary things, for they alone can reveal the true nature of reality. In Felpham, when he sees a skylark alight in front of his house, and calls it Inspiration and draws it in the shape of a woman, these two operations indicate, with the aid of a very simple example, the twofold movement of his imagination, that simultaneously changes the shape of creatures and gives them another meaning, that interprets what it clothes with another figure.

This mixture of thought and image is the fundamental characteristic of his poetic activity. There is no doubt that he sees extraordinary beings, and the strange names he gives them, and the incredible actions he credits them with acknowledge no other authority but that of an inspiration that is sure of what it receives and indifferent to all considerations of verisimilitude and logic. But far from being the product of a wandering mind, this entire set of extraordinary images expresses truths and beliefs and refers to an entire moral and religious philosophy of which the poet is profoundly aware; it is a message that can be explained, a language that must be understood, a prophesy that becomes clear if no attempt is made to translate it into purely rational terms. In other words, what Blake sees is as much the meaning as the figure, what the image means as much as the image itself, and reason just as much as appearance; and what he calls imagination has two poles: It is a twofold unbroken exchange of theoretical statement and impenetrable vision. One of several imaginary drawings by Blake that Pierre Berger singles out in his remarkable studies is "the ghost of a flea," the figure of a beastlike man with a knife in one hand and a bowl of blood in the other, which is also a representation of the military spirit and of cruelty.[5] This spirit who sucks human blood confided things to the poet that he in turn conveys to us: He told him that it was a fortunate thing for mankind that he and his like were confined to a body as small as that of a flea, otherwise they would have soon wiped humanity out. What is clear from this "vision" is that thought possesses the greatest hallucinatory power, and that it was thought that deserved to be "seen" and preserved by poetic genius.

A study of Blake's symbols and the way they develop and are enriched as they obey their own laws would run to several volumes. Except in the early poems, it is very rarely the case that allegory remains simple. Admittedly, some interpretations have emphasized the equivalences that the poet occasionally establishes between things and human passions; hence the pebble is said to equal cold, self-centered reason, the bat to equal negativity and doubt, the caterpillar to equal the pains of childbirth. But to freeze images and immobilize them within such a linear perspective is to betray the spirit of vitality and contrariness that was always the poet's ideal, while emphasizing its defects. In the symbolic poems of the first period, those that refer to contemporary events, metaphors often have their point of departure in what is visible. Berger explains, for example that if, in the song about *The French Revolution*, the Duke of Burgundy appears before the king's council to ask for the rebellions to be suppressed, it is because Burgundy is the land of vines, of flowing red wine, the wine that recalls "the great wine-press of the wrath of God,"[6] and hence the Burgundy vineyards become the symbol of bloody tyranny. In the same poem, the characters who appear to be historical express, at the human level, conflicts that take place between the Eternals. They are true insofar as they are allegorical; as walking abstractions, they must escape the limitations of the senses, and what is imaginary about them is also what makes them real. As for Blake's great legends, *The Book of Urizen*, *Milton*, and *Vala*, where in its evocations of the birth of the gods, the creation of the world and the fall of man, his prophetic spirit attains its full development, they constantly resist all efforts at exact translation or even exact interpretation, and in them, the great mythic figures are like constellations of meaning, radiant nebulae where everything is a chase, an encounter with stars, moving lights, stray lightning flashes, and bedazzled tempest. They are narratives that intentionally offend against logic: the same characters die, are reborn, or turn into others; the laws of existence are abolished, time and space no longer matter, and all that prevails is poetic magnificence and the spiritual resonances that poetry arouses in the human mind when it is regenerated by imagination.

One can have no real reservations about Madeleine Cazamian's selection. She gives pride of place to the works of Blake's youth, but the *Songs of Innocence and Experience* are a masterpiece of poetic transparency, and complete translations of them in France have been few and far between. However, alongside the *Book of Urizen* that she has translated very well and that reveals in a few pages Blake's dark grandeur, and *The Everlasting Gospel* that makes his moral and religious paradoxes accessible, it would have been desirable to include one or two of the poems drawn from the Rossetti and the Pickering manuscripts. Here, the poetry is often purer and more profound than in any other work. It is among these poems that the admirable ballad "William Bond" is to be found, containing these two verses:

> I thought Love lived in the hot sunshine,
> But O he lives in the moony light!
> I thought to find Love in the heat of day,
> But sweet Love is the comforter of night.
>
> Seek Love in the pity of others' woe,
> In the gentle relief of another's care,
> In the darkness of night and the winter's snow,
> In the naked and outcast, seek Love there!

—June 22, 1944

On the Various Ways of Dying

There is much that is memorable in Marcel Mariën's book *Weights and Measures*.[1] Some of the problems that philosophical tradition has worried away at to no avail are to be found there in a form that does not just renew them but also makes them almost attractive. Let us follow the path of a poetic author. I pick up an apple. My eye sees only its surface; my fingers touch only its exterior. Then I cut into it in order to see what is inside. What do my eyes see? Another surface; what does my hand touch? A skin, as before. The intimate heart that I am searching for escapes me, and the depths I am trying to reach are continuously absorbed by new surfaces, new images behind which they disappear. "Touch cannot reach into the true depth of objects, any better than the eye can," writes Mariën. "Their universe is in every case hermetic. If I remove the skin from an apple or the bark from a tree, what I create is a new object: for the eye, a new image has come onto the scene, for the hand, a new surface. But in neither case is what they perceive a volume."

The paradox that this expresses recalls some well-known philosophical questions. If it is a sophism, it has confounded numerous specialists, and in order to overcome it, Maine de Biran was obliged to invent a new sense, corresponding to the effort through which we become conscious of external reality in its unique inwardness. Starting from very different observations, modern psychologists also recognize original sensations that are not the product of simple contact, and that they call kinesthetic: sensations of resistance, of movement or of penetration, conveyed by muscles as they are either flexed or strained. But the psychological aspect of the problem is merely a superficial description of it. What Mariën no doubt wishes to show when he refers to unknowable depths is that we turn everything that our senses encounter into an object. To things and even to beings, we attribute an outside. We immobilize them as natures; we deprive them of any real inwardness. We look at them, and beneath our gaze, what was free consciousness turns into fixed form; the concrete object is spread out across a surface, and its thickness is merely the limit of an imaginary density. We *assume* things have an inside, but our only knowledge of them is objective and *exterior*.

"A patient visits Abernathy one day for a consultation. The celebrated doctor examines him, and says: 'You need to get some good blood into you; go and hear Grimaldi, he will make you laugh and do you more good than any medicine'.—'Good Lord,' exclaims the patient, 'I can't do that! I'm Grimaldi!'" This anecdote reveals another aspect of the same question. If all we know of others is what makes them other, we do not know what it is that others know about us. We see them as the other, they see us as the other, and the laughter we provoke, for which we as comic actors are the practiced, deliberate cause, and that consequently we "know" to perfection, is at the same time our basic ignorance, the dark side of the star, the death of our freedom. Even if such laughter makes us laugh in our turn, this marks the beginning of a new experience: The impulse that convulses me does not allow me to recoup the effects created by the faces I have pulled; I do not laugh in front of the mirror. I withdraw into myself, forever ignorant of what has become of my mimicry, the meaning it has been given, what is at stake for me when I become someone who is seen.

Mariën goes on to say: "The only death is that of the other." This is because the effect of death is to change us into a pure object. A man whom we observe has already been partly abandoned by life. For a moment, he is the prisoner of the gaze that he is subjected to. He renounces his ability to change, to exist for himself alone, to be free. He momentarily places in our hands the unforeseeable outline of his life, and already knows, in a form that is not always comfortable: the fate that will definitively be his when, after his death, his interiority will be truly exterior. When our inner voice has gone silent forever, it is then that the uninterrupted reign of others begins. Only the other has the right to speak of us. We are henceforth what others make of us, because our life has been immobilized—it has taken on its definitive shape, its account has been closed—and because we exist only in relation to others and according to the view that others have of us. This is something that Jean-Paul Sartre has expressed as follows: "Death is the triumph of the point of view of the Other over me: It transforms life into destiny. The characteristic of a dead life is that it is the life of which the other makes itself the guardian."[2]

If it is true that our gaze exerts a sort of mortal influence over people, if we live surrounded by images, hemmed in by surfaces and ignorant of any other depth than our own, it is clear how we may be led to question the value of language. True communication presupposes that we know others the way they know themselves, and that we know ourselves as though we could become strangers to ourselves. It is in this sense that Mariën talks of "a sort of transmigration of consciousnesses, a metempsychosis of the faculties that could allow us to observe and perceive the world from inside an object that is other than ourselves, in short, to experience and control a life that is alien to our own." Language provides an external reference to an inwardness that escapes us. It appears like the perpetual exterior of a deeper content that it hides as it reveals it to us. First of all, insofar as I speak for someone who is listening to me, I reveal what I am in a form that I only partly control. If I control what I want to say, I do not control the meaning that the person listening to me gives to what I say, which is an adventure about which I am never fully aware. My language for others is an irrevocable surrender; it is a game that is lost in advance, the "devil's share," say both Gide and Sartre.[3] But from another angle, even in the deepest part of me, language refers me to a truth or a reality in relation to which I am always a listener. I speak and I listen to myself: these two aspects are inseparable. As a speaker I think I am in touch with the idea, the meaning or the substance of what I am trying to express; but as a listener, I realize that all I am in touch with is a word, the letter or form, in short with a surface, a thin membrane behind which I deludedly believe that what I want to convey is concealed. As an *I* who speaks I am a free language, a freedom that expresses itself in all of its spontaneity, and as an *I* who hears, I am subject to rules that weigh me down, to syntax, grammar, and conventions that together form an order in which I am implicated, into which I am cast and where I am preexpressed and transformed at all times into a predefined object. If I die a little through being observed, while awaiting the total death that will consist in being entirely visible, I am no less perishable when, in speaking, I find myself constantly obliged to call on a dead language, and in the process of making myself understood, inter myself in a common grave.

(It remains to be said that the language in which all of the problems of a humanity without hope come to rest is also the place where hope springs eternal. Though Mariën writes very convincingly about the poverty of language, its insubstantial and inconsistent nature, though he is sad to see everything end up as words—"A book, nothing but a book," he says, "the gods themselves enjoy no better fate"—and though he shows how the most accessible texts are ruined by circumlocutions whose precision encumbers and swamps the mind, he nonetheless expresses the wish that "in human intercourse, between individuals" there should be established "a sort of voluntary rule, obliging them to reveal simultaneously with their thoughts, the detailed truth of their private behavior, and express its inner reality in its freshness and nakedness." And on the subject of clichés, *empty words*, terms that can neither retrieve nor convey what life is, here is what Jean Tardieu has written, as an epigraph to his poetic exercises in the latest issue of *Messages*:[4] "Some words are so threadbare and distended that you can see daylight through them. Immense clichés, as light as banks of fog—and as such, difficult to manipulate. But these towering empty figures, interchangeable terms that are already on the point of joining the camp of algebraic signs, finding meaning only through their place and their function, seem capable of infinite combinations, each time the mind approaches the mystery of the appearance and disappearance of objects.")

—June 29, 1944

Pages by Paul Claudel

Father André Blanchet has published a volume that brings together those pages by Paul Claudel that best reveal his thinking. What he has sought above all in these prose texts is their coherence, and the order in which he presents them to us brings together, in a logical order, insights or images about knowledge of the universe, poetic knowledge, literature and art, and finally some of the numerous commentaries inspired by the Old Testament and the Scriptures that Claudel has written in every period of his life, but particularly over the last fifteen years.[1] These extracts have been simply and carefully presented and organized, and the impression they convey is remarkable. It becomes clear not only that we no longer judge Claudel the way he was judged forty years ago, when Pierre Lasserre saw in his work "the greatest insult that has ever been directed against good sense, language and grammar," but also that what is strikingly evident today about this monumental work and this boundless author is their secret solidity, their rational coherence, and their exact proportions—in short, their triumphal striving toward order and clarity.

Paul Claudel is without doubt a free writer, who heeds his whim and is happy when he is at play. He has clearly alerted us to this himself, in joyful, good-tempered texts: "To develop an idea logically, to take pleasure in deriving the conclusion from its antecedent as if it were seen through a telescope, is something that does not happen every day for me. There are times when my mind will only proceed by fits and starts, occasionally even vanishing all of a sudden." "I have gone off fine scholastic labors, I prefer to follow my pen rather than direct it (indeed there is a certain understanding between us)." And when he defends "the rights of fantasy, whim, the incongruous, the sudden impulse and the stroke of genius," and declares "great writers were never meant to obey the laws of the grammarians, but to impose their own, and not just their will but their whim," that imperious claim expresses both the choice he has made and his natural tendency, and it mounts a defense of a language free of constraints, obedient to inspiration, responsive to the storm that rages in it, and intrepid even if it means running aground.

Commentators during the early years, whether detractors or admirers, were struck above all by this air of impetuousness. Jacques Rivière describes it as a sort of monstrosity: "Never has anyone been more monstrously a poet than you are. If you will allow me, I will say that I do not dare call you a French poet. Nothing in our literary past prepares us for your work. You land in our midst with a tremendous and unexpected violence."[2] Today, such a verdict is rather surprising: Chaos is not what we initially perceive in this work, but rather the order that chaos reveals; it is not the randomness, the verbal onslaught, the irresistible and overwhelming avalanche of images, but the form toward which these figures are oriented, the clear, commanding center that they point to, the compliance that they display throughout their twists and turns and their unusual associations. There is no text, however grandiose, where the idea does not gradually become more specific, excluding extraneous intentions, suppressing redundant developments and through its radiant sovereignty, imposing a solid, ordered structure on which each part depends. Nothing could be less obscure than Claudel's poetry and prose. At no point do they open up an abyss beneath our feet.

It is perhaps right to emphasize this impression of solidity, and ultimately of security, that we derive from the form, because it is the same impression that is provided by the spirit of the work. Obviously, as a Catholic Claudel recognizes that there are certainties. But the sort of antipathy he displays toward some of Pascal's texts draws attention to the preferences that come to him naturally. It is noteworthy that, like Valéry, he rejects the Pascalian cry: "the eternal silence of those infinite spaces strikes me with terror." "How," he says, "can one be frightened by a meadow?"[3] And elsewhere: "I will never believe that nature, in the unvarying majesty of her order, could offer us lessons in anguish and despair, the believer finds himself quite naturally in harmony with her; not because he submits to her, but because she submits to him."[4] Terror and anguish are rare in this work where God and the world do not give rise to questions, but are each in themselves firm, reasonable, and harmonious answers. And if the presence of an incomprehensible mystery, an unassailable infinity, a movement that crosses the abyss and risks being engulfed by it, constantly enlivens Claudel's metaphors, and gives them power and impetus, this is however not a mystery against which man founders but one with which he comes to terms, an infinity that accords with what is definite and that can become part of one's self, an abyss that, far from dissolving our gaze is a "fixative," as he puts it, that absorbs movement and congeals time in order to present all of its moments simultaneously to our gaze. It would seem that in order to understand the spirit of his work and gain an insight into the equilibrium it reveals, that mixture of freedom and order, risk and security, daring and caution that inspires each of its moves, we must apply to it what he himself wrote of the starry sky, the "mathematical Paradise": "It is at one and the same time a paradise and a clock, it is distance sanctified by figure, time consolidated by relations, the Infinite organized by numbers, absolute freedom within an indestructible enclosure, it is security within what is inexhaustible, it is self-evidence within mystery, it is spontaneity within fascination for the Law, it is invention within calculation, it is a soaring and a resistance, it is inextinguishable vigilance."[5] (For the same reasons, he is bothered by the art of El Greco, who at no point ever *seeks repose*, because he is a painter not of peace but of effort.)

The fact that Claudel is not a mystic, that "he is even suspicious of mystics," as Father Bruckberger has remarked, is clear from his need for the world, his liking for the world, the admirable urge he feels to embrace it, appropriate it for himself, see it and possess it with all of his senses and all of his mind. "A true poet," he says, "has no need for bigger stars or roses that are more beautiful. The ones that are there are enough for him, and he knows that his own life is too short for the lesson it provides and the approval it deserves."[6] It is this affinity that inspires his most delightful pages and his simplest images, such as those enduringly perfect ones with which *Morning Meditation* begins: "September is the gloomy month. It is neither hot nor cold. From among the brambles, Epicurus picks a large black strawberry."[7] But this universe of visible things, this solid, holy reality that, far more than dreams, illusions, or ideas, is the object of poetry, is not something that Claudel can accept in its raw splendor and its simple contingency; in fact, he is interested in it only for the meaning he can find in it, for the order he provides it with, the network of analogies, allusions, and provocations that for him constitutes the world, when it is attached to God and has become a poem, an intelligible text. "The plant is merely an image, the animal is an intention. It no longer has a place, it has a role."[8] His attitude toward the universe is thus not one of consumption or enjoyment, a boundless urge to seize hold of it. What remains of the thing he inspects? A meaning, a sign, a key, which is to say, not what is opaque and closed about it, its individual destiny, its unjustifiable singularity, but what makes it intelligible. "We are at peace and of one mind with all of nature. We are no longer afraid of animals."[9]

Neither fear nor anguish, despair, awareness of sin, nor the delirium of evil found truly new forms of expression in Claudel's work. Charles Du Bos described it as the land of joy. "Joy is the be all and end all in everything that Claudel wrote." And before all else, it is indeed a hymn; it is allied with the sun, whose prophetic profusion it celebrates, it is praise not so much in what it expresses as in what it is, not so much because of the song it sings and the arguments it presents as for its gushing power of affirmation, the prodigious and inexhaustible life that it pours forth in a glorious upsurge that is its discovery and its revelation. But is that what joy is, purely and essentially? Claudel asks himself with surprise on one occasion why so few people can sustain the thought of joy. It is perhaps because it is at the same time the height of distress, not just radiance but darkness, and that dazzling triumph of Noon, whose counterparts are the fear and the hope of an eternal Midnight.

—July 6, 1944

Narratives

What is a narrative (*un récit*)? The ridgeline of a novel? A tale told that is also true? In a narrative things are assumed to be true: Things that really happened give rise to a narrative. And then, if the narrative involves a story that is arranged and transposed, as all stories are, its development must retain a simplicity that respects the laws of the tale: as an anecdote with a beginning, a middle, and an end, it connects a series of episodes that display a straightforward verisimilitude.

Marcel Arland has called his *Zelia in the Desert* a narrative, and in so doing he helps us understand certain distinctions that are not without interest.[1] The story he offers us would seem to be connected to his childhood memories. Is it all about him? A word or a pronoun suggests that it is; we are more willing to believe what was part of someone's experience, and believing adds to the pleasure of reading. Yet, however authentic they are, memories are not enough for us. We require other elements that have perhaps been invented, perhaps observed, but whose nature is often indefinable, if our sympathy is to become more complex. We believe in an event that did happen, and if it is touching, we feel moved. But we also like to believe things that possibly did not happen, that are true without being entirely real, and that express an experience without reproducing it. The guarantee offered by memory must give way sometimes to values that free us from a belief in the past.

To say that a narrative derives its interest from the anecdote that it employs is no doubt true; but is there an anecdote that does not rely entirely on the way it is "told"? The story of Zelia may seem utterly banal: everyone knows the story of the young peasant girl who is seduced by the young lord of the manor, who loves him innocently and deeply whereas for him, she represented no more than an hour of casual pleasure; it teaches us nothing new, and we know how badly it will all end, since death must inevitably put an end to something that could never last, adding its ambiguous candor to the futile confessions we have overheard. But a story is not just the succession of little episodes it assembles, any more than a drawing is identical to the initial outline sketched on a canvas. It is thus that Marcel Arland's art displays its manifold subtlety and delicacy. A particular cadence, a landscape, a sensibility that infers without understanding, the stirrings of a season just finding its way, the marvel of a reverie inspired by a book, all of that is indicated with delicate brushstrokes, more dreamed of than known, and bathed in a dark and radiant half-light.

The first element of interest is the frame into which the narrative is inserted. The story is itself the shadow of another story, the echo of a mysterious book to which childhood once hitched its dreams, the grafting onto a delectable image of a drama that would make no sense without it. *Zelia in the Desert* is the title of an old book that the child found in the bottom of a cupboard.[2] All that he saw in this book were two engravings, one showing a girl with her eyes raised to heaven, kneeling beside her mother in an attitude of entreaty, the other in which Zelia, having reached the desert represented by a palm tree and a stretch of sand, can be seen mysteriously dreaming. The child dreams in his turn as he gazes at these images and reads the word "desert"; with a friend, he too will be able to discover a land of freedom, a secret place, secure from the prying eyes of adults. A convenient clump of pines just outside the village, a prairie shack that is mostly abandoned, offer him this story and this silence with what is the promise of a great adventure. Thus we go from book to reality, from a story barely hinted at to a more serious story that is brewing. For it is in the "desert" that the two children meet the girl, take part in the plot, and foretell its outcome.

Because this drama has two children for witnesses, and because we see it ourselves through the innocent, ignorant yet richly prescient imagination that it sets in motion, the anecdote becomes more than an anecdote: It is a landscape with clearings and murky hollows, a dance around an unknown world, a warm-hearted diversion, an intense and enlightened tragedy, in a word: a narrative. We cannot expect children to give their undivided attention to the misfortunes they have an inkling of. They obviously feel sympathy for the girl who has joined in their games, and to whose solemn guilelessness they feel drawn; they would of course like her to be happy, and they can see quite well that she is not, and they feel sad about it and perhaps somewhere they are heartbroken. But the drama surrounding them does not alter their situation. They go to school; they play; they enjoy the burgeoning spring, the festivals that take place, the maypole dance or the coming-of-age ball. For them these are also events, events filled with mirth and liveliness, in tune with their thirst for happiness, and ones that give a happy hue even to the anguish whose image they record. After all, they cannot understand everything about the tragedy: It has its dark places that they do not discover; it has its despair that they feel all the more deeply because its cause is hidden from them. And ultimately, it takes place midway between knowledge and imagination, memory and musing, and any reader who wishes to be faithful to it must go in his turn down the path of dreamy, guileless, sensual fantasy.

Without the book with its wonderful title that a child found in a cupboard there would have been no narrative, but that would have been equally the case if the first signs of spring had not made all of its episodes convincing. What is most subtle and authentic about *Zelia*, in our view, comes from the accompaniment provided by the changing light and the approaching season. At first "the air is rather chilly, rather sharp; and yet it isn't cold; the body does not shrink back, and if it will not abandon itself yet, it seems somewhere to sense a mysterious, tepid presence." Then spring is here, swift, disquieting, and ingenuous: "In fact, I don't think I have ever seen a more brutally violent springtime. The appearance of the whole village was changing: the houses, the animals, the people themselves who remained incredulous at the deep blue of the sky, the pure summer sun, those penetrating, majestic days. And as soon as daybreak came we would say 'No, it simply can't last.'" With this light, something changes, and into the "fresh mornings" and "blazing noons" there slips a grace that nothing can possibly spoil: "With the first sunbeam, long shadows, fallen from the trees and the hills, stand out against the fields. Velvet fields, spongy and golden: beneath the slanting sun, hills retreating and hoisting themselves onto the horizon, denser forests, dales and gorges that are suddenly deeper: all it took was a delicate light for this landscape, both familiar and new, to come into being before our eyes and take on life. What light, what adventure, what grace sent from heaven would one day come and grant my life those features that were still hidden within it, and that I could scarcely foresee?" Unfortunately, spring has its wiles, and though its innocence is all cajoling and flattery, it can close around the promises it brought on no less violent a whim. "Was that our spring? The fog was so dense and dull that I could hardly even make out the pear tree in the garden." With fog comes night, and with night the drama in which everything dissolves. It is impossible not to feel the softness and charm of this changing light, and how its delicacy breathes a new truth, a pure and familiar meaning into the narrative that has gracefully emerged from a child's memory, prolonged by an old book.

Last year, Dominique Rolin published an ambitious little book that displayed more presumption than it did originality. *The Marshes* described the trajectory of an ecstatic dream across the soggy terrain of traditional sentiment.[3] *Beloved Anne* is a simpler book.[4] It is the study of an unhappy woman who is drawn to bad luck, and gradually sinks deeper into a twilight zone where madness and death lurk. The book is a narrative in the sense that it confines itself to providing a series of episodes, with no other link than that provided by time as it endows them with their inevitability. These schematic twists in the story, that are sketched in rather than recounted, stand out against a horizon of anguish, a bleak, impoverished landscape. The story begins with these lines: "My name is Anne Mathias. I was drunk last night, and I fell asleep on this bench. I have just woken up. My tongue can still taste the drink they made me swallow. Around me the night is pitch black. My dress is wet, but I am going back to sleep despite the cold that makes me shiver. When I wake up again it is almost daylight." Such simplicity seems like proof of an art that is capable of moving us. The attack of this opening note, so touching in its restraint, holds out the promise of a major work that will one day perhaps be written.

—July 13–14, 1944

Léon Bloy

Albert Béguin has not only written fundamental books on fundamental subjects (taking in all of contemporary literature), such as *The Romantic Soul and Dream*, *Mysticism and Poetry*, and the like,[1] but we also have him to thank for producing a more profound conception of criticism, considered not just as an exercise of judgment but as a personal statement, a means of exploring and challenging oneself. The book he has devoted to Léon Bloy, *Léon Bloy: A Study in Impatience*,[2] certainly does deal with subjects that possess the highest personal value in his eyes, and though he has done his best to articulate and understand Bloy's views without judging them, it is clear that in the process of examining them, he comes close to something deeply personal for him. There is one very important feature of this method that stands out: You do not express yourself in relation to a work by defining it in your terms, by criticizing it and judging it from without, but by attempting to get to the heart of what it means, by accepting it entirely and unreservedly, and by adhering to it totally from within.

It is therefore to betray Bloy from the outset (though Béguin careful avoids doing so) to try and appreciate his spirit with no regard for his strictly Christian sentiments. That great writer was furiously and completely a Catholic. He lived the life of faith with unflagging rigor. His outbursts may sometimes have caused him to stray from the path of accepted, so to speak, mundane orthodoxy, but they were no worse than those for which the mystics often provide an example. He was the pilgrim of the absolute, but the absolute he went in search of with an intense passion always led him to the Church, and he accepted all of its constraints.[3] It would therefore be rather dishonest to take advantage of what was aberrant, or at least unique about Bloy's mind, in order to detach him from the only authentic mode of existence that he ever considered his own. And if it is true that his views on pain and poverty blaze a trail that some non-Christians are extending today, it is even truer that for him, they had meaning and force only within a system of faith that governed his life.

What touches us most, perhaps, is the fact that his membership of the Church did not prevent Léon Bloy from being a malcontent, and that he knew that contentment is not something we can be content with. Before all else, that is what provides the "metaphysics" of poverty and pain that he never ceased to explore. He writes to Bernard Lazare, "You have rightly seen that the Pauper is at the heart of my thinking, he is the beloved captive in my solitary dungeon. The fact is, I have nothing else to say."[4] This brings out the theme that was the fundamental theme of his existence, one that took it over in every respect and that chose him while also rejecting him. The word "pauper" must be understood in every possible sense. It would be grossly hypocritical not to stress the material aspect of poverty, the degradation it entails, the irremediable physical neglect, the mixture of abjection and misery that it causes. Poverty for Bloy is neither noble nor pure; through its association with destitution, it denotes someone who has sunk without trace. The pauper is essentially someone who has nothing to console him. He is absent and empty, and that absence and that lack fuel his desire, are the urgings of a desire that cannot be satisfied. "The pauper's desire" is in effect man himself, and it is quite clear that it only concerns man so fundamentally because it turns him to God, but it must also be said that it does not present God as fulfillment but rather as affliction, not as a refuge but as an absence of refuge in whom no solace is to be found.

In any case, one of Bloy's great assertions is that poverty is part of God himself. If he always attached the greatest importance to the Message of La Salette, it is because that message claims that God suffers now, and is thus an admission of weakness on Omnipotence's part. "*How long have I suffered on your behalf!* What a troubling, inconceivable utterance!" he writes. "The catastrophe is so immense that what is absolutely incapable of suffering suffers nonetheless and weeps. Beatitude sobs and pleads. Omnipotence declares that it cannot bear any more and begs for mercy."[5] Bloy no doubt comes up with a commentary to justify the revelation that beatitude experiences suffering. If pain is what is most profoundly human, this is because it is the reflection and the symbol of the anguish of the Son of God who, once nailed to the Cross, sees with eyes that embrace the entire history of time the "incomprehensible delays" that men impose on the work of the Holy One, and becomes aware of the protraction of his torment and the temporary failure of his designs. But the fact remains that poverty and suffering are essential to God, who is only a plenitude because he is eternally dying. Léon Bloy spoke of the wretchedness of the Holy Spirit seen as a wandering vagrant through a history that is symbolized by the misfortunes and persecutions of the Jews, and if this exile signifies hope for the Advent that will eventually happen, it also expresses the same process of thought that sees coexisting in God both greatness and wretchedness, life and death, the pinnacle and the abyss. That Omnipotence should not even be supreme satisfaction for God, that poverty, destitution and death are what lie beyond his glory, is something the author of the *Desperate Man* experienced with the same force as certain of the great mystics.[6] We may recall what Angela of Foligno said: "God gave his beloved Son such poverty that there has never been a pauper to equal him. And yet being is one of his properties. He possesses substance, and it is so absolutely his own that this belonging is beyond human words. And yet God made him poor as though substance did not belong to him" (cited in "Friendship" by Georges Bataille in an issue of *Mesures*).[7] Between the saint's words and Bloy's views the continuity is evident.

The significance of poverty is linked for Bloy not to resignation or the morose glorification of pain, but on the contrary to a sense of glory, a victorious and impassioned affirmation. This is another way in which he appeals to us. He accepts poverty, humility, and suffering, but not as virtues that he professes or ordeals that he endures. Rather, they are badges of honor that he awards himself, or a state of exuberance and triumphant elation that he attains. No one had a better sense of the relation between opposites, that for man to be torn is a joy, that his desolation is love, and that his revolt and his anger are equivalent to contemplation. "If I did not feel my wretchedness," he wrote in 1895, "how could I feel my joy, the eldest daughter of my wretchedness and who resembles her alarmingly?"[8] And in 1900: "You know neither my weakness nor my ignorance nor my real abjection nor my demonic sadness, and you know nothing of the joy that lies deep in my heart."[9] And a few months before his death: "I did not endure my wretchedness, I espoused it, out of love, even though I could have taken another wife."[10] Clearly, few writers have entrusted literature with more impassioned messages, more vehement cries or expressions of a more tempestuous and somber revolt. He who described himself as "sharing the impatience of every rebel, of all who have been let down, unanswered and condemned in this world," who at certain moments found in himself only "the bitterest and most ferocious resentment against such a harsh and unappreciative God"[11]—"I would be ashamed," he added, "to treat a mangy dog the way God treats me"[12]—yet who at the same time tirelessly expressed his mad desire for the kingdom of God ("I have such a furious hunger and thirst for the glory of God on earth," he wrote to Ernest Hello, "that I am counting the days like a madman")[13] was able to combine in a single impulse both hope and despair, spontaneous affirmation and revolt, impatience and torment with a violence, a love mixed with hate and a passion for hope and catastrophe that will long be remembered.

Many other aspects would need to be explored in order to show how Bloy is close even to those who do not accept his "mechanism of hope." Béguin objects to those critics who seek to reduce this adventure to a few biographical accidents—and it would no doubt be wrong to make too simple a link between intuition and fact in the case of this particular life. However, the important thing is that Bloy's work is indeed linked to his life, that this life constantly presents itself as being just as interesting, indeed more interesting, than all the writing in the world, and that it is the buttress and the reference point of all the books that shed light on it. It is far from irrelevant that when he was young, his father pronounced the curse, "You will always be alone," or that he had to be taken out of school "because he would attack his school friends with a knife,"[14] or that he rarely resisted an opportunity to engage in provocation, cynicism, or defiance: For example, he wrote to a scientist that he would call him Rentman because he was predestined to pay Léon Bloy's monthly rent, and to another correspondent: "You may write to your young engineer . . . that if he becomes Léon Bloy's benefactor, without changing he may allow himself the wildest follies. *This gentleman is with me*, I'll say, at the gates of Paradise. That will be enough." It is even worth observing that the young woman he was in love with and who preceded him on the road to catastrophe turned out ultimately to be a madwoman who ended her days in an asylum. Far from discrediting him, this link shows rather that Bloy was not deemed unworthy of the abyss, and that he did not speak of failure and collapse without enduring their turmoil. In addition, Bloy had a profound sense of the night, and he collided head-on with the opacity of the world. One of the last and finest pages that he wrote is a reminder of this for our contemporaries: "We are sleepers filled with half-faded images of a lost Eden, blind beggars on the threshold of a sublime palace whose doors are closed. Not only do we fail to see each other, we find it impossible to identify our nearest neighbor from the sound of his voice. Behold your brother, we are told. Ah! Lord, how could I recognize him in this faceless multitude, and how could I know if he resembles me since he is made in your image, just as I am, and I do not recognize my own face? While waiting until you deign to wake me, I have only my dreams, and sometimes they are terrible."[15]

—July 20, 1944

Poems

In a recent issue of *Poésie 44*, marking the occasion of Verlaine's centenary, Henri Thomas admired the lightness of his poetry, its ease and the skillfully balanced rhythm that turns it into song. There are also "songs" in Henri Thomas's latest collection, *Sign of Life*.[1] But whereas everything that is effortless line, fluidity of song and the harmony of simple meter, is the same wherever it occurs, the timid, startled expression he gives his melodies makes them more like those of Rimbaud, whose turn of phrase and trembling oscillations they recall. The extreme purity of style to be found in a poem like "April" must be allowed to sing for itself:

> I dream, I lose
> What little reason I have,
> I see the desert
> Deep inside the houses,
>
> Spring returns,
> What am I waiting for?

There is nothing to be plucked
From the vines of time,

Nothing, but beneath the azure
My images slumber,
The shudders of impurity,
The darkness of the foliage,

Hesitant rays,
Clouds of the days,
What does time want of me?
I have other dwelling places.

In appearance, these few lines are a restrained song that reveals itself through the movement of its cadences, and whose anxious inflexion divides and restores the confession into which we are drawn by a gently and briskly ordered rhythm. Any genre is capable of the utmost variety simply through a shift of accent, and song, however eager it is to sing in an anonymous, impersonal voice, is enriched by the infinitely diverse simplicity in which it is at home. Between Rimbaud's haughty ritornello:

Eternal Water Spirits
Divide the fine water
Venus, azure sister,
Stir up the pure wave[2]

and Verlaine's sung landscape:

The nettle and the sward
Beneath the rampart
Whence the cool sound rings
Like a shrill trumpet,
The Meuse, the drop
That we drink as we go
At each signboard[3]

there are as many differences as between these two dancing texts and the immense, mad round by Robert Desnos (which also appears in *Poésie 44*):[4]

An ant eighteen meters long
With a hat on its head,
That doesn't exist, that doesn't exist.
An ant pulling a cart
Full of penguins and ducks,
That doesn't exist, that doesn't exist.
An ant that speaks French,
That speaks Latin and Javanese,
That doesn't exist, that doesn't exist.
Hey! Why not?

A poet who is self-aware seeks to understand poetry as it relates to himself. In a few meditative lines Henri Thomas indicates how he gained access to the poetic state, the nascent state that, with no apparent changes, transforms all of the relations between a human being and the world, making them harmonious and giving them a meaning or a lack of meaning that refuses any justification. "The point where poetry is born," says Henri Thomas, "is the point where a man begins to look at what is offered him with a pleasure that borders on torpor. At this moment, between this clump of trees, this river, these crooked houses and this man, a relation has been established of a sort that makes the man wish it could last as long as possible: he could easily let it take over his life, in a state of unbounded joy." For this privileged witness there has occurred a "break in reality, and a solution to it": communication has caused a crack in the ordered, satisfying arrangement of things; sufficiency has been interrupted by it; integrity dispelled; in place of the comfortable, tranquil totality where our practical life encounters problems it can cope with, there has erupted an unstable, vertiginous movement that is like an eternal passage between two states that are constantly abolished. This situation is poetic, but it is not the poem. It is a state of sensibility that must be recaptured through an infinitely complex action whose seemingly irregular, involuntary, and fragile nature comes to an arrangement with a rigorous and coherent act, namely that of language. Between the man possessed to the point of torpor by the joy of seeing and the lucid man who assembles an ingenious system of words, rhythms, and images, what has occurred? It is this: "the current of language that passes through this man has encountered the current of tangible reality; in the fixed world, a sort of vernal debacle occurs, (in my case it is in the autumn), and the water that gives buoyancy to all things and makes them tremble is language, or more precisely, reality and language have mutually moved each other."

Hence, the emotion that arises like a whim is fulfilled as a law, and it is a perpetual oscillation between the disorder that it introduces into the world, and the coherence of the words that allow it to endure. This oscillation—the joy that disappears just as it is expressed, the anguish that evaporates when the original image that has vanished is replaced by another image, born of random words—is the hallmark of Henri Thomas's poetry. Infinitely discreet, it emerges furtively from silence, and is wary of disturbing its own contentment by confiding it. It barely touches, it spirits things away, it dissolves and survives; the sensation it has discovered is a doleful reminiscence of the chance that it never had:

> The foliage sleeps, I see,
> I listen to what increases,
>
> Words are pure sap
> The poem, a rending
>
> Of the living bough, pours forth
> A sudden rapture,
>
> Gaiety gleams beneath the leaves,
> A confusion of thirsts welcome
>
> The frenzied wave, and nothing remains
> But a horrible drought.

Every poet has his own way of being alone. For Henri Thomas, solitude is a world that is opened up for him by the unsightliness of images that have been insufficiently embraced, and where no doubt the riches he denied himself are returned to him. For Louis Émié in *The Name of Fire*,[5] it is a more crystalline universe, purged of itself, without matter, whose main substance is absence, but a burning absence, a diffuse ardor, a flame inhabited by a shadow. It is not that things do not have a place in this poetry that penetrates to their core, nor that "the call of reality" does not cohere as song in the ear of whoever chances on it. The poem about Bordeaux that begins with these lines:

> A town in the world light
> A river that is right
> To be a lovely arm folded
> Over what it youthfully confides

expresses a precise familiarity with a "geography" that is not "inhuman," with the adventure made up of air, earth and water. But it is still noteworthy that of all spectacles, the one that is most in tune with the personal experience of the poet, and that ceases precisely to be a spectacle to become an experience and an intimacy, is that of the sea, the sea playing with the day, drawing from its permanence an immeasurable capacity for metamorphosis, an infinite presence that entirely resembles absence and corresponds to the infinite sky that is revealed by the dawn:

> Fine fruit of dawn, O fires of a myriad roses,
> Are you breaking in this same garden,
> In this sea that sings its morning
> For me alone, who am already entirely yours?
>
> Streaming! It is metamorphosis . . .
> O young Azure, lucid and too human,
> It is salvation that opens in your hand
> And your rhythm in me that offers itself . . .
>
> O holy Kingdom where only light cannot go
> With its chaste excesses,
> Tree filled with gold consuming its substance,

Here is the day, delight of the living,
And the fate that regains its chance
With the gods who walk in the wind

In the grip of a disquiet that is his only real possession, a poet modifies it, transforms it and adorns it, but far from impoverishing his work, the monotony of the basic theme with which he struggles reveals the wealth of its permutations and its inexhaustible authenticity. This theme is one that each reader perceives in his own way, and extracts from it those aspects that correspond to his own anxieties. As a poetry of absence, Louis Émié's poetry can just as easily be that of a memory in search of itself, or a sign that vainly calls out to the thing signified, as the torment of the night in which we offer a voice, a presence or a reality to the shadow that haunts us:

O alive in me, O my returning dead.
I know, I see that I am your presence
And that for you I crush and drink the day

And the promise that we can bring to someone else, a spring, a birth, the language of solitude, sometimes divides into a reverie that is uncertain of itself:

Have I lost you, or are you, so dispersed,
Merely a small part of me that flees and becomes lost
In the void of your faded form?

and sometimes beguiles the world and takes on all of its glamour:

I have drowned by bones and by flesh:
My transparency absorbs me.
My face is wide open:
I am the water that walks and thinks
That it is music in the sea.

Louis Émié's poetry would not have the potency it achieves if it had not gradually acquired a strict form whose rigor is like a guarantee of the purity it aspires to. Its wealth lies in the few words that it uses, and it raises them momentarily to a power that, through the harmony of their music and their use of rhythmic conventions in which their sounds and meanings are closely bound together, restores to them all of the color, exuberance, and vitality there is to be found in the infinite sphere of the world of the senses. Language is thus "a birth and a second procreation"; and not as a restrictive rule but as proof against illusion and deceit by a false marvel, rigor prepares the soul to be greater than itself:

> Sacred Rigor, my Light and my Fire
> I strip myself bare and wait until the god
> Whose limpid language you teach me
> Comes and occupies my shape and my abode.

—July 27, 1944

The Concern for Sincerity

Yvon Belaval's book *The Concern for Sincerity* brilliantly launches Gallimard's new collection devoted to "Young Philosophers."[1] Its writing is a very successful blend of lightness and profundity. It never deals with its subject ponderously, and with no inclination to call on extraneous learning, it reveals perspectives that gradually engage the mind. In sum, it shows how the ancient tradition of French moralists, whose finest example is La Rochefoucauld, continues to inspire the most modern minds. It is a mixture of psychology and morality; its principles are implicated in its descriptions, yet they do not deflect them but rather substantiate them while leaving them pure. But these principles are a moralist's principles (and not strictly speaking those of a philosopher). That is what distinguishes this work and also makes it flawed.

There is nothing more obscure than sincerity. The first thing that strikes you about it is that it does not exist. Sincerity is not the same as frankness or veracity, nor is it the same as naturalness. To lie is not to lack sincerity: People lie about facts, about what they know to be the case and then falsify. Sincerity is more delicate, it concerns me as much as it does others, it involves an uncertain truth, it is not sure where truth lies, and expresses it without ever being certain of it. Veracity is the quality of a mind that is attentive to truth. But sincerity is not engaged in a search for just any truth: Do we ask a land surveyor if he is sincere? Sometimes error and sincerity can be reconciled; it is often when someone is mistaken that we grant him the merit of thinking sincerely. "And yet," we say, "he is sincere." As for naturalness, we take pleasure in it perhaps, we achieve it, but whether we call it ease, grace or liberty, we merely have the choice of misunderstanding it in different ways. In a study of Stendhal we observed how naturalness remained an elusive condition.[2] Belaval also quotes Stendhal: "If conversation is lively and alternating, he (the lover) can look forward to some agreeably natural moments, otherwise he will only be perfectly naturel in periods when he is less madly in love."[3] Excessive passion thus distorts what is natural: It is not enough to be sincere to avoid appearing "stiff and awkward."

Belaval finds that the first crisis of sincere conscience occurs during adolescence. Unlike the child, the adolescent no longer instinctively enjoys being part of a group: the "we" has dissolved. The adolescent feels separate from others and from himself at the very moment of discovering his inner life and that of others. He wishes to provide a true image of himself, but what is he? He goes in search of himself, he keeps an eye on himself; he observes himself in others, and in the way others observe him. Aware of the uncertainties of his nature, he dons whatever self will allow him to appear on the scene. He is both wide-eyed and affected, timid and bold, sincere out of a wish to find out who he is, and insincere out of eagerness to find himself beneath a mask that conceals him. In him, the need for sincerity is nostalgia for a lost unity, and for spontaneous communion with the group. Still unable to adapt to a reality he does not know, he appeals to rigid principles and unalloyed inner purity, and believes that way that he can secure his shifting opinions and his progress through the universe. He acts the person he is before actually becoming it. He acts it first of all in the imaginary mode, then in the presence of the privileged intermediary he calls his friend. The friend is not just a confident but an opportunity for him to know himself: in him he can discover himself, go in search of himself or express what he has not yet become. The existence of a role model is preponderant at this stage in the development of the self, but far from being a failure of sincerity, this imitation—that can take any form—is on the contrary a way of achieving it. This self-affirmation through an admired other soon allows him to affirm that he is unique. He sees himself as different, original, entirely taken up with concerns that are his alone. Naturally, sincerity has scruples; it tends to express me in what belongs exclusively to me, but it judges me too, and both denies me and refuses me. It is through anxiety and dissatisfaction that it enriches me. It offers me an ideal. Its goal is to make the society I am not part of accept me and recognize me, but only for the incommunicable truth that I have acquired.

For the adolescent, sincerity therefore has a functional value: It helps him to behave in the presence of the world of adults, and it allows him tentatively and circuitously to shape himself and get to know himself. But for many, their adaptation to adult society is always incomplete, and the juvenile crisis continues. Then the concern for sincerity changes sign, and instead of contributing to self-fulfillment, it reveals a failure, the uneasy experience of the failure of socialization. Rousseau appears: "Myself alone. I feel my heart and I know men. I am not made like any I have seen; I venture to believe that I was not made like any that exist. If I am not deserving, at least I am different."[4] The sincere man remains immune to the reality against which he protests. Unskilled in the use of social techniques, he resorts to a sort of purist magic through which he aims to obtain and even demand the indulgence of others. I am sincere, and this sincerity must totally suffice. I am truthful, and this global, fundamental truthfulness can dispense me from any more concrete truth, or else allow me to master it from the outset. In the sincere man there is a menacing reliance on a power that is his to use: sincerity gives him rights, and these rights are limitless, because a conscience that is tormented, proud of its torment and capable of revealing it, brings out in all other men the bad conscience that dwells in them. And once again this recalls Rousseau: "Eternal being . . . let each of them, here on the steps of your throne, in turn reveal his heart with the same sincerity; and then let one of them say to you, if he dares, *I was better than that man*."[5] In short, says Belaval, by using an emotional technique, the sincere man seeks to break out of the solitude to which both his reflections and his weakness have confined him. He dreams of a return to an original "we," but he is content just to dream it. He is beguiled by his scruples, he speaks only to himself and of himself, he fails and he rejoices in his failures. His analyses are merely autopsies of the past. They make him into a faltering, bitter being.

Sincerity presupposes self-knowledge, but it posits that this knowledge can never be complete. For it, "I am" does not possess a rigorously expressible meaning; the expression must always be improved upon, always found wanting. Sincerity is essentially disquiet, anguish, the awareness of a lack: it is a search for an elusive harmony, an impossible conformity with oneself. These are strange features that invite us to enquire about their origin, and even to wonder how sincere consciousness is even possible. This is something Belaval does not tell us, and that is why, however discerning and interesting it may be, his thinking sometimes appears unclear. He compares the concern that he is analyzing to the instinct for fabulation that is so active in children. The child plays with the imaginary. It applies its imagination to the world where the real matches up to its desires; it involves itself through fable. Fabulation can thus be seen as the origin of insincerity. No one will be content with this psychological explanatory principle, or at any rate see it as a first explanatory principle. How could consciousness be capable of this imaginary behavior, simultaneously believing and not believing what it is, becoming separate from itself and at the same time coinciding with itself? It is noteworthy that many of the features that Belaval has used to describe sincere consciousness were first used by Sartre to describe the structure of consciousness in general. Consciousness is a lack, it perpetually escapes itself, transcends itself in view of an inaccessible given, and is obsessed with an absence that always causes it to fail. What is striking is that sincere consciousness is as it were an enchantment of consciousness by itself: it claims to locate value (that is to say, what provides an absolute foundation) in the movement of disintegration, in the flight and the incompletion it knows itself to be; it wants to communicate with others by plunging deeper into a subjectivity with which it is fascinated; it emerges from itself when it attaches itself to itself (to its possibilities only, but to all of its possibilities). Sincere consciousness believes that its innermost freedom is self-evident. It believes that its particular movement can be grasped from without, without being transformed into a stable given. It observes itself and believes it has been seen. To be sincere is to have a strong idea of one's own absence, the better to be present for others; it is see one's liberty as an end in itself (and consequently to deplete it and betray it), in order to impose it on the freedom of others.

—August 3, 1944

No Man's Son

Henri de Montherlant has published his latest play, *No Man's Son*, accompanied by a detailed commentary.[1] He thinks people will find such a large number of marginal notes ridiculous. But why? There are two sorts of writers: those who do not offer an interpretation of their works, because they do not consider that they are better placed than any reader to do so (Paul Valéry is a case in point); then there are the authors who comment on themselves both out of mistrust for people who read and out of interest in what they write. That is all perfectly normal. The level of misunderstanding that accompanies a given work is always considerable. A man of letters who explains himself will perhaps manage to limit the damage; five times out of ten, what he says will produce further misreadings, and these misreadings will give rise to others, but these explanations will result in a brief moment of truth that will shed some passing light on the play.

"A drama of human quality," is how Montherlant describes *No Man's Son*. "A father rejects his son—and his rejection perhaps sends him to his death—because the son is of poor quality." And this is indeed the apparent subject. Young Gillou has all of the faults that the writer generally attributes to people of mediocre quality. He is nice but spineless; his main weakness is that he is interested in film stars, reads comic books, sings silly songs, and wipes his shoes on the lining of a curtain (in a villa that does not belong to his family: "What's the problem? It don't belong to us"). He is a little cowardly, a little evasive, a little affectionate. Nothing about him is precise, nothing clear-cut; as an individual he is robustly insipid and flat, "as flat," says his father, "as his flat hair and his pasty, flabby features." His father loves him dearly, but he cannot abide this mediocrity. In the end, he sacrifices him to his idea of what a man should be, to his personal morality that the child offends against and contradicts.

What makes the play appear highly questionable is the fact that this father who speaks in the name of human quality is himself of mediocre quality. When he chides his son for his petty approach to things, his worship of false values and his instinctive animosity toward true ones, it is evident that he is appealing to principles he himself does not observe. Naturally, we find his behavior beyond reproach: the fact that he abandons his mistress after fathering her child, then twelve years later, meeting mother and child by chance, feels a pang of fatherly nostalgia and wants to look after this unknown son, are honest, robust, and perfectly legitimate impulses that have nothing to do with "an ethic of quality." It is what he is—and what he says—not what he does, that is petty and mediocre. He is solemn, sententious, and singularly lacking in good humor, that good humor that is the sign of quality and generosity (a sad heroism is a worthless heroism). There is something of the Joseph Prudhomme about him: "My experience," he says, "my culture . . ." and elsewhere: "As for me, I tell you the only people I can bear nowadays have to be rather superior. All my life I have made sure that I had no idiots, or almost no idiots around me." This is a highly comical observation, because the mistress he has chosen is an extremely stupid, vulgar, feeble woman, who thinks his son is very intelligent because "out of everyone in the house . . . he is the one who knows how to use the ration book." There is nothing spontaneous, nothing animated about this most uncomprehending of fathers. If he studies his son, it is in order to fill a notebook with advice, rules for living, and comments about his character: he believes that an educator has performed his task when he has written down one or two general truths, or uttered sentences of this variety: "Memory has nothing to do with judgment, it is the intelligence of the idiot." Inept he certainly is, but being inept is just the half of it, he is also vain like a pedant, and just as blinkered. The art of living totally escapes him. Then comes an incident that reveals him for what he is: He has forbidden his son to buy lottery tickets. Why? Because it is stupid and because it is immoral. Fine. But then he added: "If someone gave him a national lottery ticket, he would give it to a beggar rather than keep it: it would dirty his hands." In other word, this affluent lawyer does not want to dirty his hands, yet what is degrading to him seems perfectly appropriate for a beggar. He could tear up his ticket or give it to one of his own sort, but no way. It is for a beggar that he keeps it, for someone of inferior quality for whom anything that is worth something is no longer worth anything. His "to a beggar" is the cracked sound produced by inferior metal.

Montherlant argues that this father does not represent the ideas of the author, and we believe him of course. But where has the play gone? If we find ourselves confronted with three equally mediocre characters, if the father is merely a man with bad instincts who confuses vanity with pride, inflexibility with rigor, the petty disdain people get bogged down in with the grand disdain that comes from love; if the mother is a pretentious birdbrain who loves her son like a sentimental machine; and if the son is "a snotty-nosed kid," chances are that the drama of "human quality" will disintegrate into a series of misunderstandings of which no one is aware and that leads nowhere, because the outcome of a play is only tragic if the characters are worthy of interest, but insignificant people are of no interest at all. What makes this work an ambiguous one is that it hovers between what its author wanted it to be and what it actually is. For its author, it is the drama of human quality: a father who has his faults but who has a sense of quality sacrifices his son to this ethic because he is unworthy of it. For us it is a totally different drama: one of unconscious misunderstanding, for the father sacrifices his son to an ethic of which he is totally unaware and that he betrays himself, much more than his son does, through his obtuseness and his lack of spiritual refinement. He is therefore duped, and everyone else along with him.

It remains to be seen whether this ethic of quality we are told of can be expressed, and whether it is not betrayed as soon as it is spoken of. The lawyer's main defect is that he transforms into an ethic and into principles what is only significant if it lies beyond ethics. He appeals to a rule that that is not a rule, and that in any case requires us not to appeal to it, and never to see it as a rule. He says: this ethic of mine. That expression alone is enough to prove his inferior quality. There is no one baser or more culpable than a man who preaches in the name of silence, and turns the loftiest enigma into a banal cliché.

—August 10, 1944

The Magical Experience of Henri Michaux

There are many aspects of Henri Michaux's very varied, rare and important work that deserve to be noted. But almost simultaneously he has published a new collection with the title *Exorcisms*, and a selection of pages drawn from his previous works whose title and tendency point us toward the part of himself that the author wishes us to be aware of.[1] *The Space of Inside* is also a collection of exorcisms.[2] It is a series of tableaux that evoke a magical experience. Whether in depictions, tales, poems, or incantations, this experience is expressed using literary methods that are extraordinarily effective but do not have a literary goal.

The word "magic" occurs frequently in Henri Michaux's work. He entitled one of his works *In the Land of Magic*, and several of its pages also contain the word.[3] But if a whole section of his work can be seen as an effort of magical consciousness, the revelation of a magical reality, it must immediately be noted that the term he uses does not have the vague and hackneyed sense that usually suffices in everyday use. Magic is something other than a power of enchantment, and it places extraordinary resources at mankind's disposal.

"I write as best I can," says Michaux, "the first time in response to a wager or rather a fit of anger. I was very surprised by the result of the explosion that was dubbed a poem. It happened again. I have still not got used to it. I write in a state of abandon, and for myself." A significant part of his work is marked by this presence of violent emotion. Anger gives it the form of a perpetual act of aggression, a wily or impetuous struggle, a defensive reaction against an object that is itself endowed with malice, and is aggressive and mindlessly cruel. ("In fact," he notes when he describes the "movements of inner being,"[4] "a person who does not know anger knows nothing. Knows nothing of what is immediate.") What anger has built, anguish or fear destroys. Building is dizzying, instantaneous, a sort of cataract, a surge that is so powerful that it triumphs instantaneously over the insignificance of its means. (An essential theme in Michaux is the theme of the builder. The builder appears absurd because he builds with anything whatsoever; but the point is he *can* build with anything whatsoever. He is the master of a world that has no time for the virtues of expediency; he is capable of what he feels: "I'll build you a town with rags, I will! With no plans and no cement, I'll build you a building that you will be unable to destroy.")[5] But slowly, patiently, anguish ruins the edifice of spontaneity and tempest in advance, nullifies it before it can exist. It is the dark night of encumbrance, the indefinite projection of disorder and precariousness. Everything always has to be done again, everything disappears, and death itself, as in the Hindu view, is merely the promise of an endless new beginning. ("In this universe, there are few smiles. Whoever enters it experiences an infinite number of encounters that wound him. However, no one dies there. If you die, everything begins again.")[6]

It is because it is the direct product of emotion that Michaux's world is a magical one. Through emotion we try to find a way into a world that is no longer governed by reasonable, entirely determined relations, but by magic. Anger, for example, is a form of magical behavior that tends to strike down with a single blow a person or a thing that we do not have the time to engage in real combat. The real world is too difficult, too slow. Anger will not wait. It does not have the patience to follow the winding pathways that promise real action. It will therefore blank out every practical consideration, and the concrete act of vengeance will be replaced by a symbolic action, a magical action consisting of gestures, threats and words through which, outside of time, it will take place in all the fury of its desire. This marks the beginning of a new relationship between man and the world. But it is just the beginning. For as soon as things lose their rational, clearly defined structure, they take hold of the consciousness that has given rise to them and force it into exhausting captivity. In order to be rid of a hateful world that offends it, anger plunges into a world of encumbrance that it can never get the better of. How terrible objects are for Michaux, full of unparalleled aggression, inexhaustibly vicious and ferocious. It is because he himself, in his anger, has constructed a world of hostility out of them, a rampart of ferocity and malice that is endlessly collapsing and endlessly being rebuilt. And this is no imaginary projection. That is exactly how the world of emotion is, clamping itself around consciousness, engulfing it little by little, closing it in on itself and convincing it that it is a permanent prisoner, and that imprisoned in this way, it can only call on incantatory means to defend itself, means that free it momentarily but at the same time drive it even deeper, by binding it intimately to the magical world it aims to be free of by becoming more and more magical. ("Our inner being is continually fighting gesticulating larvae. Suddenly, it finds itself emptied of them as if they were a cry, or debris swept away by a sudden hurricane. But the invasion soon begins again from below.")[7]

Michaux's world is one of both unpredictable spontaneity and infinite inertia. Spontaneity and passivity are the two features of the magical world. Consciousness is lost among things.

It has itself become a thing. It is henceforth without limit or form. It still tends in the direction of a sort of finality, but it achieves this by absolute means. Simultaneously, everything is possible: That is the illusion of the inward-looking being who realizes everything he imagines—and nothing is possible, for, trapped in the density of matter, the mind is nothing but transfixed patience, indifference to the abyss, a viscous dough that will no longer rise. The extreme objectivity of *A Certain Plume*, *Journey to Great-Garabagne*, and *In the Land of Magic* expresses this tragic aspect of consciousness, whose intimacy, instead of being lived and perceived from within, is contemplated from without, lives in an open world, and is no more than a spectacle that refers to nothing. In all of these works there is an extraordinary effort—one of the most significant of our time—to express man through the absence of man, to describe the world of human reality by creating a world where man can no longer recognize himself, and by imagining a human point of view that is entirely alien to man. That is also the anguished dream of magical consciousness. It seeks to escape itself, and it can only do so by presenting itself with a world where it constantly encounters itself. It tries to go beyond itself, and for it, to go beyond itself is to spread itself about everywhere, become dissolved in everything and be even where it is not.

If Henri Michaux's inventions appear so close to us and affect our fate, even when they seem to involve nothing that is ours, it is first of all because they symbolize the general condition of our destiny that dictates that it can only find a meaning for itself through an effort to escape that meaning, indeed any meaning whatsoever—so that it is the gratuitous nature of his fables and sometimes of his language that we consider most important. But at the same time, this gratuitousness, this muted objectivity, this deaf and blind placidity belongs to a movement that at its other extreme is a raging, tempestuous power, anxiety and despair, infinite emotion. There is no contemporary body of work in which human anxiety and failure are expressed so reservedly and so violently and have found a prouder and more tragic voice. How could anyone forget *My Properties*, *Darkness Moves*, or *A Certain Plume*, in which we hear the grave and solemn complaint of poems such as "Death Song"? "Fortune once again, fortune with its oily tongue after washing my wounds, fortune like a hair that you take and try to braid with your own, having taken me and joined me indissolubly to her, suddenly as I was already wallowing in joy, suddenly Death came and said: 'It is time. Come.' Death forevermore Death now."[8]

—August 17, 1944

A Chronology of the "Chronicles of Intellectual Life" Collected in *Faux pas*

1941

"The Silence of Mallarmé," *Journal des Débats* (hereafter *JD*), April 23, under the title "Le biographe connaît le 'génie' et ignore l''homme'"; *Faux pas* (hereafter *FP*), 99–106.

"The New Novel," *JD*, May 14, under the title "Le jeune roman"; *FP*, 183–186.

"The Birth of a Myth," *JD*, June 9–10; *FP*, 192–195.

"The Criticism of Albert Thibaudet," *JD*, June 23–24; *FP*, 283–287.

"The Solitude of Péguy," *JD*, June 30—July 1; *FP*, 279–282.

"The Novel and Morality," *JD*, July 14–15; *FP*, 234–238.

"The Art of the Novel in Balzac," *JD*, July 21–22; *FP*, 177–182.

"Chaminadour," *JD*, August 4–5; *FP*, 227–233.

"Léon-Paul Fargue and Poetic Creation," *JD*, August 25–26; *FP*, 147–151.

"The Secret of Melville," *JD*, September 1–2; *FP*, 239–243.

"Alain's Thinking," *JD*, September 11; *FP*, 301–305.

"The Angel of the Bizarre," *JD*, October 7; *FP*, 222–226.

"Goethe and Eckermann," *JD*, November 11; *FP*, 269–272.

"How Is Literature Possible?" *JD*, November 25, December 2; *FP*, 76–84.

"Kierkegaard's *Journals*," *JD*, December 23; *FP*, 17–22.

1942

"On Insolence Considered as One of the Fine Arts," *JD*, January 6; *FP*, 306–312.

"Literature," *FP*, January 20; *FP*, 91–98.

"Mythological Novels" (first part), *JD*, January 27, 3 under the title "Littérature"; *FP*, 196–199.

"Bergson and Symbolism," *JD*, February 10; *FP*, 112–115.

"On Hindu Thought," *JD*, February 17; *FP*, 33–36.

"Is Mallarmé's Poetry Obscure?" *JD*, February 24; *FP*, 107–111.

"The Marriage of Heaven and Hell," *JD*, March 25; *FP*, 28–32.

"The Silence of Mallarmé," *JD*, April 1; *FP*, 99–106.

"The Enigma of the Novel," *JD*, April 8; *FP*, 187–191.

"The Novel and Poetry, *JD*, April 22; *FP*, 203–207.

"A Work by Paul Claudel," *JD*, April 29; *FP*, 288–295.

"Reflections on the New Poetry," *JD*, May 27; *FP*, 128–131.

"The Baroque Poets of the Seventeenth Century," *JD*, June 3; *FP*, 122–127.

"Molière," *JD*, June 10; *FP*, 259–262.

"Lamartine's Position," *JD*, July 22; *FP*, 152–155.

"Poetics," *JD*, August 5; *FP*, 116–121.

"The Novel of the Stranger," *JD*, August 19; *FP*, 217–221.

"Stendhal and Sensitive Souls," *JD*, August 26; *FP*, 263–268.

"Mythological Novels (second part)," *JD*, September 2, under the title "De l'humour romanesque"; *FP*, 199–202.

"Poetry and the Novel," *JD*, September 30, under the title "Romans et souvenirs"; *FP*, 208–211.

"An Edition of *Flowers of Evil*," *JD*, October 7, under the title "Une edition critique des *Fleurs du mal*"; *FP*, 156–164.

"Master Eckhart," *JD*, November 4; *FP*, 23–27.

"On the Subject of *The Fruits of the Earth*," *JD*, November 11; *FP*, 296–300.

"The Myth of Sisyphus," *JD*, November 25; *FP*, 53–58.

"Involuntary Poetry," *JD*, December 9, under the title "Oeuvres poétiques," paragraphs 4–7; *FP*, 132–134. For the rest of this article, see *Desperate Clarity*, 182–187.

1943

"André Gide and Goethe," *JD*, February 3; *FP*, 273–278.

"Studies on Language," *JD*, February 10; *FP*, 85–90.

"Rilke," *JD*, March 10; *FP*, 47–52.
"The Notebooks of Leonardo da Vinci," *JD*, March 24; *FP*, 71–75.
"Inner Experience," *JD*, May 5; *FP*, 37–41.
"The Experience of Proust," *JD*, May 12; *FP*, 42–46.
"Chaminadour" (second part), *JD*, May 19, under the title "De l'oeuvre de M. Jouhandeau"; *FP*, 231–233.
"The Myth of Orestes," *JD*, July 27; *FP*, 59–64.
"A Work by Paul Claudel," *JD*, August 11, under the title "Études sur Paul Claudel"; *FP* (in part), 288–295.
"The Myth of Phaedra," *JD*, August 18, under the title "Lecture de Phèdre"; *FP*, 65–70.
"Poetry and Language" *JD*, September 1; *FP*, 135–140.
"After Rimbaud," *JD*, September 15; *FP*, 141–146.
"Mallarmé and the Art of the Novel," *JD*, October 27; *FP*, 165–171.

Notes

INTRODUCTION BY MICHAEL HOLLAND

1. Maurice Blanchot, *Faux pas* (Paris: Gallimard, 1943), trans. Charlotte Mandell (Stanford: Stanford University Press, 2002). For a detailed chronology of the texts contained in *Faux pas*, see the end of this volume.

2. For a discussion of this theme, see pages 9–12 of my introduction to Blanchot's *A World in Ruins: Chronicles of Intellectual Life, 1943* (New York: Fordham University Press, 2016).

3. For example, in "For Friendship" (1996) Blanchot refers to "the shock mixed with irritation" that he felt on learning that Gallimard was to publish *Faux pas*. See Maurice Blanchot, *Political Writings, 1953–1993*, trans. Zakir Paul (New York: Fordham University Press, 2010), 134.

4. Following a misunderstanding over Blanchot's intentions regarding his future with the *Débats*, three of the four chronicles for December 1943 appeared on the front page. Once this was cleared up, it was agreed that from now he would have a slot on pages 2 and 3 of the paper, but also that his chronicles would be reduced in length by about 40 percent.

5. In the diaries he wrote during the occupation years, the lawyer Maurice Garçon paints an unflattering portrait of the *Débats* and its director, Étienne de Nalèche. See *Journal (1939–1945)* (Paris: Les Belles Lettres/Fayard, 2015), 96–97, 367, 374–375.

6. In an intriguing development, in 1943 and then on two occasions in 1944, Blanchot's chronicles attracted the attention of Charles Maurras in *L'Action Française*. Commenting on "Charles-Louis Philippe" (see *A World in Ruins*, 43–50), Maurras observed: "in the field of contemporary literature I know of no wilder [*plus effréné*] Kamchatkan than M. Maurice Blanchot" (*L'Action Française*, February 24, 1943). This obscure epithet no doubt alludes to the critic Sainte-Beuve's description of Baudelaire's work as a "bizarre kiosk" situated "at the far tip of the Romantic Kamchatka [*à la pointe extrême du Kamtchatka romantique*]." Perhaps because of Thierry Maulnier's admiration for Blanchot's novels, which he reviewed in *L'Action Française* on January 28 and November 26, 1942, Maurras admitted in 1944 to a certain admiration for Blanchot's criticism, and on January 10, and then again on May 30, 1944, he evoked "the most distinguished Kamchatkan" for his articles "The Mystery of Criticism" and "A Secret Tone" (see "Sainte-Beuve and Baudelaire" and "The Kamchatkan's Amazement [*Le Kamtchatkane émerveillé*]." His admiration is lukewarm, however. Summing up the claim made in "The Mystery of Criticism" that the critic's only mode can be silence, Maurras dismisses it as "a stream of words devoted to incoherent fancies." And in an article entitled ". . . et noctium phantasmata" ("The Fears and Terrors of the Night") (*L'Action Française*, July 29, 1944, 2), François Daudet reflects the true opinion of Maurras's circle when he dismisses "the 'neo-poetical' twaddle and obscure contortions of M. Maurice Blanchot" (*les billevesées "néo-poétiques" et les obscures tortillons de M. Maurice Blanchot*") in his article "Poems."

7. See Blanchot, "The Writers' Silence," in *Into Disaster: Chronicles of Intellectual Life, 1941* (New York: Fordham University Press, 2013), 13–17.

8. The first piece he published after the war was an extract from his novel *The Most High*, which appeared in 1948. See "Le Tout-Puissant," *La Table Ronde* 3 (July 1945): 187–198.

9. Michel Surya, "Présentation," in Georges Bataille, *Discussion sur le péché* (Paris: Lignes, 2010), 30–31.

10. See Jean Lescure, *Poésie et liberté: Histoire de Messages, 1939–1946* (Paris: Éditions de l'IMEC, 1998), 181–182. I examine this scene in more detail in "Bataille, Blanchot and the 'Last Man'," *Paragraph* 27, no. 1 (March 2004): 50–63.

11. See "Chateaubriand's Secret" in this volume.

12. See *A World in Ruins*, 4.

13. Maurice Blanchot, letter to Francis Ambrière, March 29, 1944. In Fonds Francis and Madeleine Ambrière, Bibliothèque de l'Institut, Paris (MS 7943, Correspondance de guerre).

14. Christophe Bident, *Maurice Blanchot: Invisible Partner*, trans. John McKeane (New York: Fordham University Press, 2017).

15. Maurice Blanchot, *The Instant of My Death*, in Maurice Blanchot and Jacques Derrida, *The Instant of My Death/Demeure: Fiction and Testimony*, trans. Elizabeth Rottenberg (Stanford: Stanford University Press, 2000), 5. Blanchot's story is also published separately in an unpaginated translation by Cid Corman (Green River, VT: Longhouse Publishers & Booksellers, 2002).

16. See the letter to Maurice Nadeau dated April 17, 1977, which Nadeau published in the *Quinzaine littéraire* 741 (June 16–30, 1998), 5. It is in "Two Letters to Maurice Nadeau," trans. Michael Holland, in "Blanchot's Epoch," *Paragraph* 30, no. 3 (November 2007): 18.

17. This episode forms the basis of the brief narrative entitled *The Instant of My Death* that Blanchot published in 1994. See note 15. A degree of uncertainty surrounds the precise details of this event. Coincidentally, the chronicle that appeared on the same day is entitled "On the Various Ways of Dying."

18. In April, the clandestine publication *Bibliographie de la France* (a parallel publication to the official publication of the same name) issued a warning to readers under the heading "A l'Index" to exercise "particular vigilance" with regard to the publishers Denoël, Stock, and Grasset. In July, the clandestine newspaper *Libération* issued a similar warning, directed this time at a list of publishers that now included Gallimard ("Avis à MM les éditeurs," July 10, 1944).

19. Dominique Fernandez recounts the episode in 1943 when Marguerite Duras told her neighbor, Fernandez's father Ramon, that she and her husband Robert Antelme had joined the Resistance, despite the fact that Fernandez was openly a collaborator. He concludes his anecdote with a reference to the staircase of the block in the rue Saint-Benoît where both Duras and Fernandez lived, "on

which, during the dark years, regardless of the political divide, all those engaged in the life of the mind would encounter each other." See Dominique Fernandez, *Ramon* (Paris: Grasset/Livre de Poche, 2008), 30.

20. On March 22, the main airfields in France were bombarded, and on May 1 the principal railway stations were the targets. The bombing campaign reached a peak in May, with 1,284 raids in that month alone, causing thousands of civilian deaths. See Philippe Buton, "La France atomisée," in *La France des années noires*, vol. 2, *De l'Occupation à la Libération*, ed. Jean-Pierre Azéma and François Bédarida (Paris: Seuil, 1993), 377–404, and André Brissaud, *La dernière année de Vichy* (Paris: Librairie Académique Perrin, 1965).

21. It was responsible for the murders of Victor and Hélène Basch in January, Jean Zay in June, and Georges Mandel in July. Mandel was killed in retaliation for the assassination in June of Philippe Henriot, the Vichy Minister of Information and Propaganda, by members of the Resistance.

22. See Tzvetan Todorov, *A French Tragedy: Scenes of Civil War, Summer 1944*, trans. Mary Byrd Kelly (Lebanon, NH: University Press of New England, 1996).

23. Max Weber, "Politics as a Vocation" (1919), in *Essays in Sociology* (London: Routledge, 1991), 78.

24. Ibid.

25. On June 10, the SS murdered 642 inhabitants of the village of Oradour-sur-Glane in reprisal for the murder of a German officer, even though the commanding officer had ordered that a much smaller number be executed (thirty or fifty, depending on the account). Similar acts of unbridled violence occurred in Tulle, Ascq, Ugines, and elsewhere. And the deportation of Jews continued at an increased pace; between February and May, 11,000 Jews were deported. Even in the face of defeat, the Nazis persisted with their destructive goal until August 1944.

26. Jean Guéhenno, *Diary of the Dark Years*, trans. David Bell (Oxford: Oxford University Press, 2014 [1947]), 29 (translation modified).

27. Jean Guéhenno, once again: "We know that our fidelity is not futile. Through this fidelity, thanks to it, France survives in this disaster, in this shame, in this chaos. And if we are faithful enough, perhaps in a year, two years . . . Europe, exhausted by its very disor-

der, may model itself on France, on a certain high, pure idea of man that a few men will never once have compromised." Ibid., 61 (translation modified).

28. For a discussion of the significance of this notion for Vichy, but also for de Gaulle in 1944, see Debbie Lackerstein, "*La France éternelle*: A Contested Ideal, Vichy and the Present," in *French History and Civilization: Papers from the George Rudé Seminar* (2015), 6:292–302.

29. Careful analysis of Blanchot's prewar political journalism would establish that the move contained in the title of his first article in *L'Insurgé*, "From Revolution to Literature," is predicated on the conviction that what "France" has so far signified for him as a Catholic nationalist has ceased to be a viable political entity. *L'Insurgé* 1 (January 13, 1937), 3. Numerous articles in *L'Insurgé* assert what he calls "the terrible paradox that obliges [the French] to be French against France, national against the nation." "The Only Way to Be French," *L'Insurgé* 22 (June 9, 1937), 4. His penultimate political article, "France, a Nation to Come," makes explicit his conviction that France has ceased to exist, while preserving the hope that it will one day rise again. *Combat* 19 (November 1937): 131–132. However, by discrediting both sides of the distinction made by Charles Maurras between "Legal France" (the Republic) and "Real France" (the Nation), this article situates the France of the future entirely outside of any existing political frame, in a future that is a pure hypothesis. By 1944, that hypothesis no longer holds: The future has collapsed into an endless "now," and outside is revealed to lie nowhere. Blanchot's prewar political texts have recently been published under the title *Chroniques politiques des années trente* (Paris: Gallimard, 2017).

30. See, for example, Maurice Blanchot, *The Space of Literature*, trans. Ann Smock (Lincoln: University of Nebraska Press, 1982 [1955]), 106; and *The Infinite Conversation*, trans. Susan Hanson (Minneapolis: University of Minnesota Press, 1993 [1969]), 120.

31. As he said of his involvement with "Jeune France." See Blanchot, "For Friendship," 135.

32. See "After Rimbaud," in *Faux pas*, 144.

33. Jean-Paul Friedrich Richter had a vision of his own death on November 15, 1790, which formed the cornerstone of much of what he would go on to write. See Jean Paul Friedrich Richter, *Ideen-Gewimmel*, 236. See also Edgar Allan Poe, "The Facts in the Case of Mr Waldemar," and Franz Kafka, *The Hunter Gracchus*.

34. The last words of the 1951 *récit* entitled *When the Time Comes*—whose French title, *Au moment voulu*, is one translation of Nietzsche's "Stirb zur rechten Zeit"—are "Now, the end." See Maurice Blanchot, *When the Time Comes*, trans. Lydia Davis (Barrytown, NY: Station Hill Press, 1995), 74. See also Friedrich Nietzsche, *Thus Spoke Zarathustra*, trans. R. J. Hollingdale (Harmondsworth: Penguin Books, 1969), 97.

THE MYSTERY OF CRITICISM

1. Ramon Fernandez, *Itinéraire français* (Paris: Éditions du Pavois, 1944).

2. Jean Paulhan, *Les fleurs de Tarbes* (Paris: Gallimard, 1941). Blanchot reviewed this work in three separate articles in the *Journal des Débats* in 1941. Two of them were published as *Comment la littérature est-elle possible* (Paris: Corti, 1942); "How Is Literature Possible?" trans. Michael Syrotinski, in *The Blanchot Reader*, ed. Michael Holland (Oxford: Blackwell, 1994), 49–60. The third, "Terror in Literature," is to be found in Maurice Blanchot, *Into Disaster*, trans. Michael Holland (New York: Fordham University Press, 2013), 101–106. The reference to Fénéon is from Jean Paulhan, "F.F. ou le critique," *Confluences* 26 (November 1943): 547–557.

3. Taken from Georges Bataille, *L'expérience intérieure* [1943], in *Oeuvres complètes* (Paris: Gallimard, 1973), 5:153.

RETURN TO THE SOURCE

1. Lanza del Vasto, *Le pèlerinage aux sources* (Paris: Éditions Denoël, 1944); *Return to the Source*, trans. Jean Sidgwick (London: Rider, 1971; New York: Schocken Books, 1972).

FROM ONE NOVEL TO ANOTHER

1. Christian Megret, *En ce temps-là* (Paris: Plon, 1943).

2. Henryk Sienkiewicz, *Quo vadis?* trans. B. Kozakiewicz and J. L. de Janasz (Paris: Éditions de la Revue blanche, [1896] 1901); *Quo Vadis: A Tale of the Time of Nero*, trans. S. A. Binion and S. Malevsky (New York: H. Atlemus, 1897); Louis Bertrand, *Sanguis martyrum* (Paris: Fayard, 1918).

3. Louis Parrot, *Le grenier à sel* (Marseille: Robert Laffont, 1943).

4. Raoul Dujardin, *L'enfant sage* (Paris: Flammarion, 1943); Jean Milo, *L'esprit de famille* (Paris: Denoël, 1943).

THE FOUR GOSPELS

1. *Les quatre Évangiles*, trans. Hubert Pernot (Paris: Gallimard, 1943).

2. Marie-Joseph Lagrange, *A Catholic Harmony of the Gospels* (London: Burns, Oates & Co., 1930).

3. Marcel Jousse was a Catholic priest who became one of the foremost anthropologists in the interwar years. He was a pupil of Marcel Mauss, Pierre Janet, and Georges Dumas and was known for his theory that language has its origin in gesture. James Joyce attended some of his lectures and refers to him in *Finnegans Wake* when he writes "In the beginning was the gest he jousstly says" (468.05). Quoted in Stephen Heath, "Ambiviolences," in *Post-Structuralist Joyce*, ed. Derek Attridge and Daniel Ferrer (Cambridge: Cambridge University Press, 1984), 55–56.

4. Matthew 13:56. This and all other quotations from the Bible are taken from the New American Standard Bible.

5. Paul Mazon, *Introduction à l'Iliade* (Paris: Belles Lettres, 1942).

FROM JEAN-PAUL TO GIRAUDOUX

1. Jean Paul Richter, *Vie de Fixlein, régent de cinqième*, trad. Pierre Velut (Paris: Aubier-Montaigne, 1943); in *Army-Chaplain Schmelzle's Journey to Flaetz and Life of Quintus Fixlein*, trans. Thomas Carlyle (Columbia, SC: Camden House, 1991).

2. Jean Giraudoux, *L'école des indifférents*, in *Oeuvres romanesques complètes* (Paris: Gallimard, 1990), 1:154.

A DIARY WITHOUT EPISODES

1. Raymond Dumay, *L'herbe pousse dans la prairie* (Paris: Gallimard, 1941). Blanchot reviewed this novel in 1941. See "Two Novels," in *Into Disaster: Chronicles of Intellectual Life, 1941* (New York: Fordham University Press, 2013), 23–26.

2. Raymond Dumay, *Mon plus calme visage* (Paris: Gallimard, 1944), first published in Algiers in 1942; *Le printemps des hommes* (Paris: Gallimard, 1944).

3. Jean Giraudoux, *Adorable Clio* (Paris: Émile-Paul, 1920).

ON THE SUBJECT OF LANGUAGE

1. Albert Dauzet, *La géographie linguistique* (Paris: Flammarion 1944).

2. Jules Gilliéron, *Atlas linguistique de la France* (Paris: Honoré Champion, 1902–10).

3. Jean Paul Sartre, *Being and Nothingness: An Essay on Phenomenological Ontology*, trans. Hazel E. Barnes (London: Methuen, 1957), 516.

THE ROMANCE OF MADEMOISELLE AÏSSÉ

1. The original title of the article, "Le roman d'Aïssé," could have been translated as "The Novel of Aïssé." I opted for the title of the novel that Mrs. Campbell Praed published in 1910, since it captures more precisely the nature of what Blanchot describes. Interestingly, two years after this, Jérôme and Jean Tharaud published a volume entitled *Le roman d'Aïssé*, whose subject was not, however, the woman known as Aïssé, but the relations between Anna de Noailles and Maurice Barrès. Jérôme and Jean Tharaud, *Le roman d'Aïssé* (Paris: Éditions Self, 1946). Was Blanchot aware that this book was in preparation? Or did the Tharaud brothers read his chronicle?

2. See Charles-Augustin Sainte-Beuve, "Mademoiselle Aïssé," *Revue des Deux Mondes* 13 (January 15, 1846); also in *Portraits littéraires*, vol. IV.

3. *Les lettres d'Aïssé*, ed. Marcel Arland (Paris: Stock, 1944).

THE JOY OF STORYTELLING

1. Marcel Aymé, *La vouivre* (Paris: Gallimard, 1943); *The Fable and the Flesh*, trans. Eric Sutton (London: Bodley Head, 1949).

2. Marce Aymé, *Les contes du chat perché* (Paris: Gallimard, 1968); *The Wonderful Farm*, trans. Norman Denny (London: Bodley Head, 1952); *Return to the Wonderful Farm*, trans. Norman Denny (London:

Bodley Head, 1954). Aymé published his *contes* over a period of twelve years, between 1934 and 1946. The two volumes of *The Wonderful Farm* contain a selection of them.

OUTLAWED IDOLS

1. André Berne-Joffroy, *Présence de Valéry, précédé de Propos me concernant* (Paris: Plon, 1944).

THE ART OF ANDRÉ DHÔTEL

1. For Blanchot's review of *Le village pathétique*, see *A World in Ruins: Chronicles of Intellectual Life, 1943* (New York: Fordham University Press, 2016), 138–139.
2. André Dhôtel, *Nulle part* (Paris: Gallimard, 1944).

BALZAC'S WAY OF WORKING

1. André Billy, *Vie de Balzac* (Paris: Flammarion, 1944). The quotation by Théophile Gautier is from "Honoré de Balzac," in *Oeuvres complètes de H. de Balzac* (Paris: A. Houssiaux, 1855), 1:1–16; that from Balzac is from a letter to Madame Hanska, 1837.

THE GOTHIC NOVEL

1. Horace Walpole, *Le château d'Otrante*, trans. Dominique Corticchiato (Paris: José Corti, 1943).
2. Maurice Heine, "Promenade à travers le roman noir," *Minotaure* 5 (May 1934): 3.

THE SECRETS OF THE DREAM

1. See André Breton, *Communicating Vessels*, trans. Mary Ann Caws and Geoffrey T. Harris (Lincoln: University of Nebraska Press, 1990), 131–132.
2. Luc Durtain, *Les secrets du rêve* (Paris: Flammarion, 1944).
3. "*Wenn sich ein Mensch entschließen könnte, alle seine Träume ohne Unterschied, ohne Rücksicht . . . niederzuschreiben, so würde er*

der Menschheit ein großes Geschenk machen" (*Tagebücher*), cited by Freud in his *Interpretation of Dreams*.

4. Paul Valéry, "Introduction to the Method of Leonardo da Vinci," in *The Collected Works of Paul Valéry*, Vol. 8, *Leonardo, Poe, Mallarmé*, trans. Malcolm Cowley and James R. Lawler (London: Routledge, 2007), 86.

5. "*Des données immédiates*," a phrase that refers to Henri Bergson's work *Essais sur les données immédiates de la conscience* (1889), whose English translation is *Time and Free Will: An Essay on the Immediate Data of Consciousness* (New York: Dover, 2001).

A NOVEL BY JARRY

1. Alphonse Daudet, *Tartarin de Tarascon* (Paris: E. Dentu, 1887); *Tartarin of Tarascon*, trans. J. M. Cohen (London: Folio Society, 1968).

2. Henri Monnier, *Mémoires de M. Joseph Prudhomme* (Paris: Librairie Nouvelle, 1857).

3. Charles Doury, "Alfred Jarry," *Gil Blas* 1237 (November 3, 1907): 1.

4. Louis Lormel, "Alfred Jarry: Souvenirs" (1907), *L'étoile d'absinthe* 39–40 (1988): 26.

5. Ibid.

6. Alfred Jarry, *Le surmâle* (Paris: Éditions de la Revue Blanche, 1902), 221); *The Supermale*, trans. Barbara Wright (London: Jonathan Cape, 1968), 108–109 (translation modified). Quoted in André Breton, *The Lost Steps*, trans. Mark Polizzotti (Lincoln: University of Nebraska Press, 1996), 36.

7. Jean Giraudoux, *Provinciales* (Paris: Bernard Grasset, 1909).

8. Alfred Jarry, *La dragonne*, ed. Jean Saltas (Paris: Gallimard, 1943); *The She-Dragon*, trans. Dr Faustroll, in *Pataphysica* 2 and 4 (New York: iUniversal, 2004, 2006), 1–50, 1–123.

NOVELLAS AND STORIES

1. For Blanchot's review of Claude Roy's *Suite française*, see *A World in Ruins: Chronicles of Intellectual Life, 1943* (New York: Fordham University Press, 2016), 141–147.

2. Claude Roy, *La mer à boire* (Paris: Sequana/René Julliard, 1944). The French title literally means "having the sea to drink up" and evokes a common expression "*ce n'est pas la mer à boire*," meaning "it isn't asking the impossible," or more commonly "it's no big deal."

3. Marcel Béalu, *Mémoires de l'ombre* (Paris: Gallimard, 1944).

CHATEAUBRIAND'S SECRET

1. Louis Martin-Chauffier, *Chateaubriand ou l'obsession de la pureté* (Paris: Gallimard, 1943).

2. Chateaubriand, letter to Mademoiselle Adèle de . . . , June 6, 1829.

FANTASTIC NOVELS

1. Robert Poulet, *Prélude à l'apocalypse* (Paris: Éditions Denoël, 1944).

2. Noël Devaulx, *Le pressoir mystique* (Neuchâtel: Les Cahiers du Rhône, 1942).

3. Villiers de L'Isle Adam, *L'Ève future* (Paris: M. de Brunhoff, 1886); *Tomorrow's Eve*, trans. Robert M. Adams (Champaign: University of Illinois Press, 2000).

4. René Barjavel, *Le voyageur imprudent* (Paris: Éditions Denoël, 1944).

AIR AND DREAMS

1. See "Fire, Water and Dreams," in Maurice Blanchot, *Desperate Clarity: Chronicles of Intellectual Life, 1942* (New York: Fordham University Press, 2013), 152–158. Gaston Bachelard, *L'air et les songes* (Paris: Corti, 1943); *Air and Dreams: An Essay on the Imagination of Movements*, trans. Edith and Frederick Farrell (Dallas: Dallas Institute of Humanities and Culture, 1988).

2. Friedrich Nietzsche, *Poésies,* 232.

3. "On the Spirit of Gravity," in Friedrich Nietzsche, *Thus Spoke Zarathustra*, trans. Adrian del Caro (Cambridge: Cambridge Texts in the History of Philosophy, 2006), 153.

4. Bachelard, *Air and Dreams*, 250 (translation modified).

JOYCE'S FIRST NOVEL

1. Louis Gillet, *Stèle pour James Joyce* (Marseille: Éditions du Sagittaire, 1941); *Claybook for James Joyce*, trans. Georges Markow-Totevy (New York: Abelard-Schuman, 1958).

2. James Joyce, *Dedalus: Portrait de l'artiste jeune par lui-même*, trans. Ludmila Savitzky (Paris: Gallimard, 1943); *A Portrait of the Artist as a Young Man* (London: Penguin Classics, 2003).

A SECRET TONE

1. Gillet, *Claybook for James Joyce*, 39.

2. This is an allusion to *Donner à voir* by Paul Éluard (Paris: Gallimard, 1939).

3. Marcel Lecomte, *L'accent du secret* (Paris: Gallimard, 1944).

THE LITERARY *I*

1. Franz Kafka, *Diaries, 1910–1923*, entry dated September 19, 1917, trans. Martin Greenberg (New York: Schocken Books, 1949), 183–184.

2. Marcel Jouhandeau, *De l'abjection* (Paris: Gallimard, 1939); *Chroniques maritales* (Paris: Gallimard, 1938); *Les miens* (Paris: Gallimard, 1942); *L'oncle Henri* (Paris: Gallimard, 1943).

CHARLES CROS

1. Charles Cros, *Poèmes et proses* (Paris: Gallimard, 1944).

2. Charles Cros, *Le coffret de santal* (Paris: Alphonse Lemerre, 1873).

3. Charles Cros, *Le collier de griffes* (Paris: Stock, 1908).

THE BIRTH OF ROME

1. Georges Dumézil, *Naissance de Rome: Jupiter, Mars, Quirinus. II* (Paris: Gallimard, 1944). For Blanchot's review of Dumézil's *Jupiter, Mars, Quirinus*, see *Desperate Clarity: Chronicles of Intellectual Life, 1942* (New York: Fordham University Press, 2013), 92–98.

WILLIAM BLAKE

1. William Blake, *Poèmes choisis* (Paris: Aubier, 1943).

2. William Blake, letter to Butts, July 6, 1803.

3. In English in the original. Yeats's actual words were "a too literal realist of the imagination," in "William Blake and his Illustrations to the *Divine Comedy*" (1897), *Ideas of Good and Evil* (London: A. H. Bullen, 1903). Northrop Frye shortened the phrase to "literalist of the imagination," in *Fearful Symmetry: A Study of William Blake* (Princeton: Princeton University Press, 1947), 85–107. Marianne Moore uses the phrase in "Poetry": "when dragged into prominence by half poets, the / result is not poetry, / nor till the poets among us can be / "literalists of / the imagination"—above / insolence and triviality and can present / for inspection, "imaginary gardens with real toads in them," shall / we have / it" (Marianne Moore, *Selected Poems* (New York: Macmillan, 1935).

4. William Blake, "The Everlasting Gospel" (1818), in *The Poetry and Prose of William Blake*, ed. David V. Erdman (Berkeley: University of California Press, 2008), 555.

5. See Pierre Berger, *William Blake, Poet and Mystic* (London: Chapman & Hall, 1914).

6. Revelation 14:19.

ON THE VARIOUS WAYS OF DYING

1. Marcel Mariën, *Les poids et les mesures* (Brussels: Éditions des Auteurs Associés/La Boétie, 1944).

2. This single quotation is made up of two separate sentences from Sartre's *Being and Nothingness*. The first is quite significantly truncated compared to the original: "Death . . . is the triumph of the point of view of the Other over the point of view *which I* am toward myself. This is doubtless what Malraux means when in *Days of Hope* he says of death that it 'transforms life into destiny.'" Jean-Paul Sartre, *Being and Nothingness: An Essay on Phenomenological Ontology*, trans. Hazel E. Barnes (London: Methuen, 1957), 540. The second is grammatically incomplete and has been rectified (ibid., 541).

3. See André Gide, *Journals*, trans. Justin O'Brien (Urbana: University of Illinois Press, 2000), 2:225; Jean-Paul Sartre, *Being and*

Nothingness, 265. Barnes uses the expression "devil's part" rather than "devil's share."

4. Jean Tardieu, "Deux mots nuls," *Messages* 1 (January 1944); "De la dignité considérée comme un obstacle," *Messages* 2 (April 1944).

PAGES BY PAUL CLAUDEL

1. Paul Claudel, *Pages de prose* (Paris: Gallimard, 1944).

2. Letter dated December 1, 1910, in Jacques Rivière and Paul Claudel, *Correspondance 1907–1914* (Paris: Plon, 1926), 222.

3. Claudel, *Pages de prose*, 68.

4. Paul Claudel, *Positions et propositions* (Paris: Gallimard, 1934), 138.

5. Blanchot uses this same quotation in "A Work by Paul Claudel," in *Faux pas*, trans. Charlotte Mandell (Stanford: Stanford University Press, 2001), 294. The original article appeared in the *Journal des Débats* as part of "Études sur Paul Claudel" on August 11, 1943.

6. Paul Claudel, "Introduction à un poème sur Dante" (1921), in *Oeuvres en prose* (Paris: Gallimard, 1965), 423 ff.

7. Paul Claudel, *L'épée et le miroir* (Paris: Gallimard, 1939).

8. Paul Claudel, *L'art poétique* (Paris: Mercure de France, 1951 [1907]), 156; *Poetic Art*, trans. Renee Spodheim (New York: Philosophical Library, 1948), 101.

9. Paul Claudel, *Du sens figuré de l'Écriture* (Paris: Desclée de Brouwer, 1938).

NARRATIVES

1. Marcel Arland, *Zélie dans le desert* (Paris: Gallimard, 1944).

2. Marguerite Daubenton, *Zélie dans le desert* (1787).

3. Dominique Rolin, *Les marais* (Paris: Denoël, 1942). For Blanchot's review of this novel, see *Desperate Clarity: Chronicles of Intellectual Life, 1942* (New York: Fordham University Press, 2013), 111–113.

4. Dominique Rolin, *Anne la bien-aimée* (Paris: Denoël, 1944).

LÉON BLOY

1. Albert Béguin, *L'âme romantique et le rêve* (Paris: Corti, 1939); *Gérard de Nerval, suivi de poésie et mystique* (Paris: Delamain et Boutelleau, 1936).

2. Albert Béguin, *Léon Bloy l'impatient* (Fribourg: Egloff, 1944); *Léon Bloy: A Study in Impatience*, trans. Edith M. Riley (London: Sheed and Ward, 1947).

3. See Léon Bloy, *Le pélerin de l'absolu* (Paris: Mercure de France, 1914); *Pilgrim of the Absolute*, trans. John Coleman and Harry Lorin Binsse (London: Eyre & Spottiswood, 1947).

4. Letter to Bernard Lazare dated October 1892, in Léon Bloy, *Journal inédit I. 1892–1895* (Lausanne: L'Âge d'Homme, 1896), 232.

5. Léon Bloy, *Le fils de Louis XVI* (Paris: Mercure de France, 1900), 34.

6. Léon Bloy, *Le désespéré* (Paris: A. Soirat, 1886).

7. Dianus (a pseudonym of Georges Bataille), "L'amitié," *Mesures*, April 15, 1940, 132; also in *Oeuvres complètes* (Paris: Gallimard, 1973), 6:293. Bataille does not quote Angela of Foligno directly, and his version differs from the one used by Blanchot.

8. Léon Bloy, *Le mendiant ingrat: Journal de l'auteur, 1892–1895* (Paris: Robert Laffont, 1999), 1:153.

9. *Journal*, January 1900, letter to "un bienfaiteur ingrat."

10. March 6, 1917, reply to a letter from an unknown correspondent (Alfred Loeuwer) who had sent him 50 francs, *La porte des humbles* (Paris: Mercure de France, 1920), 236.

11. Léon Bloy, *Le désespéré*, 181.

12. *Journal*, 19 September 1879, Letter to Ernest Hello. Joseph Bolléry, *Biographie de Léon Bloy* (Paris: Albin Michel, 1947) 1:428–429.

13. Letter to Ernest Hello, March 22, 1880, in ibid., 1:424.

14. Cited in Jean-Louis Galet, "Les années périgourdines de Léon Bloy," in *Léon Bloy*, ed. Michel Aubry (Lausanne: l'Âge d'Homme, 1990), 56.

15. Léon Bloy, *Dans les ténèbres* (Paris: Mercure de France, 1918), 34–35.

POEMS

1. Henri Thomas, *Signe de vie* (Paris: Gallimard, 1944).

2. Arthur Rimbaud, "Comédie de la soif" (1872).

3. Paul Verlaine, "Du fond du grabat" (1881).

4. Robert Desnos died in the Theresienstadt concentration camp on June 8, 1944.

5. Louis Émié, *Le nom du feu* (Paris: Gallimard, 1944).

THE CONCERN FOR SINCERITY

1. Yvon Belaval, *Le souci de sincérité* (Paris: Gallimard, 1944).

2. See "Stendhal and Sensitive Souls," in Maurice Blanchot, *Faux pas*, trans. Charlotte Mandell (Stanford: Stanford University Press, 2001), 267. This article first appeared with the title "Stendhal et les âmes sensibles" in *Journal des Débats*, August 26, 1942, 3.

3. Stendhal, *De l'amour*, I, xxiii.

4. Jean-Jacques Rousseau, *The Confessions*, trans. Angela Scholar (Oxford: Oxford University Press, 2000 [1782]), 5.

5. Ibid.

NO MAN'S SON

1. Henri de Montherlant, *Fils de personne* (Paris: Gallimard, 1944); *No Man's Son*, trans. Jonathan Griffin, in *The Master of Santiago and Four Other Plays* (London: Routledge & Kegan, 1951), 175–232.

THE MAGICAL EXPERIENCE OF HENRI MICHAUX

1. Henri Michaux, *Exorcismes* (Paris: R.-J. Godet, 1943).

2. Henri Michaux, *L'espace du dedans* (Paris: Gallimard, 1944).

3. Henri Michaux, *Au pays de la magie* (Paris: Gallimard, 1941); "In the Land of Magic" (extracts), in Henri Michaux, *Selected Writings*, trans. Richard Ellman (London: New Directions, 1968), 237–270. For Blanchot's review of this work, see *Desperate Clarity: Chronicles of Intellectual Life, 1942* (New York: Fordham University Press, 2013), 99–105.

4. Henri Michaux, "Mouvements de l'être intérieur," in *Plume* (Paris: Gallimard, 1938).

5. Henri Michaux, "Contre" (1934), in *La nuit remue* (Paris: Gallimard, 1935); *Darkness Moves: An Henri Michaux Anthology*, trans. David Ball (Berkeley: University of California Press, 1997).

6. Henri Michaux, "La nuit des embarras," in *Plume*.

7. *L'espace du dedans*.

8. Henri Michaux, "Chant de mort," in *Plume*; "Song of Death," in Henri Michaux, *Selected Writings*, 75 (translation modified). Blanchot omits the comma in the last sentence between "Death" and "forevermore," which changes the overall sense subtly.

Index